The Rise & Fall

of

Dr. Russell H. Carrington Jr.

A Novel Based On A True Story

Russell H. Carrington IV

The Perfect Smile

Illustrations
All illustrations appearing in this work are original charcoal renderings created specifically for this publication. These illustrations are interpretive artistic works inspired by family recollection and historical context and are not reproductions of photographs.

For permissions or inquiries, contact:

IV Legacy Media Publishing, LLC

3028 Greenmount Ave.

Baltimore, MD 21218

ISBN: 979-8-218-71629-5

Printed in the United States of America

First Edition: [January, 2026]

"Brothers of the professional life, you can't win it all"

- Reverend Ernest P. Clark

Dr. Russell H Carrington Jr.

"The Perfect Smile"

A Novel Based On A True Story

The Rise and Fall of Dr. Russell Carrington Jr. is a gripping biographical drama that delves into ambition, sacrifice, and the consequences of personal choices. Set in the 1970's, the novel masterfully explores Dr. Carrington's rise in the medical field while exposing the familial and societal pressures that shaped his fate. The vivid storytelling and historical depth make for an engaging read, revealing the complexities of success and downfall. A compelling mix of drama and intrigue, this book is a must-read for fans of character-driven narratives.

- **Baltimore Best Reviews**

"The Rise and Fall of Dr. Russell H. Carrington Jr." effectively highlights its exploration of themes such as abandonment, betrayal, and the struggle for acceptance faced by African American men in their homes, schools, and societies. I describe it as a "page-turner," emphasizing its engaging plot and emotional depth. The focus on determination and resilience showcases the challenges Dr. Carrington and others endure in their pursuit of success. Overall, the book offers a powerful reflection on identity and perseverance, making it a significant read that resonates with its audience.

- **Dee Pope**

Acknowledgments

Writing The Perfect Smile has been a journey of uncovering not just one man's story, but the complex layers of family, legacy, and identity that shaped him. I am deeply grateful to those who helped bring this narrative to life.

First and foremost, I thank the Carrington family—those still with us and those who live on through memory—for their courage, honesty, and grace in sharing personal histories. Your willingness to revisit the past made this work possible.

To my research advisors and historical consultants, thank you for helping me navigate the nuanced social and medical landscapes of 20th-century Baltimore. Your insight helped anchor this story in truth.

I owe sincere appreciation to my editors, proofreaders, and early readers, who challenged me to refine every chapter while honoring the emotional core of the story.

To the mentors, teachers, and peers who encouraged me to keep writing when the weight of the subject matter felt heavy—your words gave me strength.

Finally, to anyone who has ever struggled with the expectations placed on them, with the meaning of success, or with the quiet battles within a family—I wrote this for you.

— Russell H Carrington IV

Dr. Russell H. Carrington Jr. Dental Office

IV Legacy

CONTENTS

Introduction

In the sad evening skies of Baltimore, 1972, the world of Dr. Russell Hubert Carrington Jr. was poised to collapse. The man once hailed as the city's prodigal son—a dental virtuoso with charm as precise as his scalpel—now stood on the precipice of scandal. Beneath the polished veneer of his success laid secrets, ambition, and betrayal that threatened to crack the perfect smile he had spent his life perfecting.

From his first steps onto the campus of Morgan State College in 1950, his brilliance was undeniable. He was a man who demanded attention, who carved his destiny with the precision of a craftsman and the vision of a dreamer. By the time he opened his state-of-the-art dental practice in Baltimore, he had seemingly outrun the ghosts of his past.

And yet, perfection is a fragile thing. Behind his success lay an insidious truth: Dr. Russell Hubert Carrington Jr. was a man torn between ambition and integrity, between love and self- preservation. As his personal and professional worlds collided, the cracks in his flawless façade began to show.

This is the story of a man who dared to dream beyond the boundaries, who built his empire on charm and brilliance, and who watched it all crumble beneath the weight of his own contradictions. It is a story of resilience, betrayal, and the human cost of chasing perfection.

Welcome to *The Perfect Smile.*

"The Rise and Fall of Dr. Russell Hubert Carrington Jr."

Based On A True Story

PART 1

Chapter 1

On The Hills Of Rosemont

Born on May 11, 1932, to Genevieve Estelle Preston—a fiercely independent 24-year-old woman—Russell Jr.'s arrival marked the beginning of her unwavering resolve to keep her child, despite her family's insistence that she consider other options. On the other hand, Russell Hubert Carrington Sr. was a man torn between societal expectations and his burgeoning love for Genevieve and their son. Though he made no excuses for his failings, he could not bring himself to defy his parents, whose influence loomed over every decision he made.

The Carringtons and Prestons came from vastly different worlds. The

Carrington family had long been established as one of Baltimore's respected Black families. They were descendants of free Black artisans and landowners dating back to the 19th century. Their wealth, though modest by white society's standards, was significant within their community, allowing them to live comfortably after relocating from the Belair, Maryland farmland to a stately, all-brick row home in a prosperous Black neighborhood.

The Carringtons prioritized education and respectability, holding firmly to the belief that proper decorum and adherence to societal norms were key to advancement. Russell Sr. was a strict but fair man who worked in the pharmacy at the University of Maryland Hospital. His position not only provided financial stability but also made him a figure of authority within the community. However, their emphasis on tradition and social status created an unyielding expectation— particularly for Russell Jr.—to excel and uphold the family's legacy.

In contrast, the Prestons rose to prominence not through inheritance but through sheer determination and strategic connections. Russell Jr.'s mother was the daughter of a skilled domestic worker who catered to wealthy white families and learned the intricacies of their world. Genevieve's mother used her knowledge of etiquette and social diplomacy to build a network of influence within both the Black and white communities.

Genevieve herself carried this skillset into adulthood, earning a reputation as a masterful hostess and an advocate for Black women's advancement. Through her involvement in civic organizations, charity drives, and church activities, the Prestons cemented their reputation as leaders who uplifted their peers.

While Genevieve dressed impeccably and cultivated an air of refinement, much of the family's social standing relied on their active community engagement and Genevieve's ability to project an image of prosperity. Her unparalleled ability to blend into spaces where Black families were often excluded became her greatest asset. With charm, intelligence, and cultural awareness, she forged connections with influential figures, positioning her family as a symbol of upward mobility. She was often the first to volunteer for leadership roles in church and charity events, ensuring that the Preston name became synonymous with dignity and service.

Despite the tension surrounding his arrival, Genevieve poured all her ambitions and unfulfilled dreams into her son. She doted on young Russell Jr. and worked tirelessly as a seamstress, determined to give him the best education and every opportunity she could afford. His father, though not present in the traditional sense, provided steady financial support, ensuring that his son would bear the Carrington name.

As Russell Jr. grew, he carried the weight of both his parents' dreams. His mother taught him resilience and self-reliance, while his father's success and power cast a long shadow of expectation. These formative years shaped the man he would become: ambitious, fiercely intelligent, and determined to craft a legacy that would make both families proud.

By the time Russell Jr. turned eight, the contrast between his two worlds became undeniable. Genevieve did everything she could to shield him from the whispers of neighbors and the judgment of her own family. The stigma of being a single mother in 1940s Baltimore clung to her like a shadow, but she refused to let it define her son's future. She instilled in Russell Jr. a fierce determination, often telling him, "You are not defined by where you come from but by where you choose to go."

Genevieve Estelle Preston married Sam Fields, becoming Mrs. Genevieve Fields. Sam, a practical and dependable man, provided stability and support to both Genevieve and Russell Jr. Though Sam treated Russell Jr. with kindness, their relationship was never particularly close. Despite this emotional distance, Sam's influence instilled in Russell Jr. a sense of discipline and perseverance—traits that would serve him well in achieving his future goals.

Meanwhile, Russell Sr. remained a steady, albeit strict and firm, presence in young Russell Jr.'s life. Every Sunday, Genevieve would dress her son in his Sunday best and take him to his father's family church, Metropolitan Methodist Church, located in West Baltimore at the corner of Lanvale and Carrollton Avenue. His uncle, the Reverend Napoleon Bonaparte Carrington, pastored the church.

Russell Sr. was no ordinary man. A cornerstone of the Rosemont community in Old West Baltimore, he was one of the first Black men to integrate the neighborhood—a pioneer breaking barriers in a time when such progress demanded exceptional courage and determination. Beyond his personal achievements, the Carrington family played a pivotal role in shaping West Baltimore's spiritual and cultural identity, helping to bring African churches into the heart of the community and creating spaces for faith and fellowship to thrive.

The family's influence extended beyond the church pews and into the pressroom of the *Afro-American Newspaper*, where their steady hands and sharp minds contributed to one of the nation's most respected Black publications. The Carrington elders stood as symbols of dignity and professionalism. The men of the family were known for their sharp suits and even sharper minds. Many, including Russell Sr., were proud 32nd-degree Masons—part of a fraternity of Black professionals who wielded their influence to uplift their community.

Being surrounded by powerful Black men planted seeds of ambition in Russell Jr. He observed the fine suits his father wore, the car he drove, and the air of authority he carried. It wasn't just the material wealth that captivated him—it was the power, the respect, and the way others seemed to receive his father with such deference. Though Russell Jr. didn't yet have the words to articulate it, he vowed that one day, he too would command that same presence.

In school, Russell Jr. excelled. His sharp mind and quick wit made him a favorite among teachers. He buried himself in books, particularly those on science and medicine.

By the time he entered high school, Russell Jr. had already decided he wanted to become a dentist. It was a profession that combined precision, skill, and prestige—a perfect match for his temperament and ambitions. He attended Frederick Douglass High School, which was established for African Americans and located in the heart of West Baltimore City. Originally named the "Colored High School" in 1883, it held a proud legacy as a cornerstone of Black education.

As a teenager, Russell Jr. was painfully aware of the barriers society placed before him. He internalized every slight and setback, learning over the years to shield himself with perfection—a pristine image that left no room for error or vulnerability.

In private, however, he would replay every criticism, every distant whisper of disapproval. The weight of becoming Dr. Russell Carrington Jr.—brilliant, charismatic, untouchable—was a burden that felt almost unbearable at times.

This duality made him both fascinating and dangerous. His sensitivity fueled his brilliance, driving him to extraordinary heights, yet it also left him exposed and vulnerable. By the time he was 18, Russell Jr. was already carrying the heavy weight of expectations far beyond his years. He was the son of a proud family, with a future that seemed as bright and limitless as his ambition. But all of that changed with one mistake—or what his family deemed a "mistake."

Russell Jr. met the beautiful Frances Lokeman. Frances, a Lake Clifton High School senior, was the daughter of a well-respected family. Sweet and soft-spoken, she had a quiet charm. Her light skin, shapely figure, and freckled face only added to her allure. Their youthful indiscretions, however, had consequences neither could have foreseen.

Like his father, Russell Jr. reveled in fleeting romances, charming his way into the hearts of many but committing to none. When Frances's mother discovered that she was pregnant, the fallout was swift and unforgiving.

Russell Jr. and his childhood best friend, Donald Stewart, walked the cracked sidewalks of West Baltimore, their schoolbooks tucked under their arms. The afternoon sun stretched their shadows along the rowhouse-lined street.

"She's pregnant, Donald." Russell Jr.'s voice was low, uncertain. "Frances is having my baby."

Donald sucked his teeth, shaking his head. "Damn, Russ. That's heavy." He paused, glancing over at his best friend. "What you gonna do?"

Russell Jr. exhaled sharply, running a hand over his neatly combed hair. "I don't know, man. My father already thinks I'm wasting my time with her. Now this?" He kicked at a loose stone in the pavement. "I can't get stuck here, Donald. You know that."

They climbed the marble steps of Russell Jr.'s rowhome, dropping onto the cool stone. The city hummed around them—kids playing in the alley, a radio spilling Sam Cooke's voice from a nearby window, the distant rumble of a streetcar.

Donald leaned back on his elbows. "You always said we were getting outta here. Morgan State. Dental school. A real shot." He looked at Russell Jr. "This don't gotta change that."

Russell scoffed. "You sound like it's that easy."

"Nah," Donald admitted. "But you ain't the first man to be in this spot. Question is, you gonna let it stop you?"

Russell Jr. stared at the chipped paint on the railing, his mind racing. His whole life, he'd been chasing something bigger than West Baltimore—the lectures his father drilled into him, the dreams he whispered to himself late at night. And now?

He rested his elbows on his knees, clasping his hands together. "I just—" He hesitated. "I don't wanna be like my old man. Cold. Calculating. But I can't throw everything away, either."

Donald nodded slowly. "Then don't. But you gotta figure out what kind of man you wanna be, Russ. 'Cause that baby? That's real. And so is your future."

They sat in silence for a while, watching the world move around them—two boys on the edge of manhood, caught between duty and ambition.

Russell Jr. was given no choice. His family, eager to avoid scandal, demanded he "do the right thing." Her family, desperate to preserve their daughter's honor, insisted on marriage.

And so, with trembling hands and a heavy heart, Russell Jr. stood before the altar, pledging vows he didn't yet understand to a woman he hardly knew.

Chapter 2

In His Fathers Shadow

The birth of their child, Russell Hubert Carrington III, brought joy, but it also tethered Russell Jr. to a life he felt unprepared for. He loved his son—there was no question about that—but beneath the surface, resentment simmered. He had been forced to set aside his dreams, his independence, and his vision of a life unencumbered by obligation.

Over time, the strain of marriage became unbearable. Russell Jr. buried himself in his studies, chasing success as if it could erase the choices he had been forced to make. The pressure to provide, combined with his unresolved bitterness, drove a wedge between him and his wife, turning their marriage into a battleground of unspoken regrets and unmet expectations.

The weight of that forced union began to shape Russell Jr. in ways he couldn't have anticipated. He resented how his life had been derailed at such a young age, how his dreams had been sacrificed at the altar of duty. Rather than confront these feelings, he buried them deep, allowing them to calcify into a quiet bitterness that would later seep into every aspect of his life.

His wife, though devoted, bore the brunt of his frustration. She had hoped the birth of their son would bring them closer, but it only seemed to push him further away. Russell threw himself into his studies and future, determined to rise above his circumstances. For him, success became more than ambition—it became redemption. The brighter his star burned, the more he could distance himself from the shadows of his past.

Despite his growing emotional distance, Russell Jr. took pride in providing for his family. He made sure his wife and son wanted for nothing, believing that material comfort could compensate for his absence. But the cracks in their marriage deepened. The woman who had once admired his brilliance began to see the cold detachment lurking behind his polished charm.

By the time Russell Jr. achieved the success he had always dreamed of, their relationship had become little more than a formality. They lived in separate homes and inhabited separate worlds. She clung to the hope that the man she had fallen in love with might one day return, while he justified his neglect as the price of greatness.

For Russell Jr., the marriage became a painful reminder of everything he had lost—freedom, control, and the ability to dictate the terms of his own life. That resentment, coupled with his growing hunger for power and recognition, set the stage for the moral compromises and personal betrayals that would ultimately lead to his fall.

As the years passed, Russell Jr. grew increasingly detached from his wife, the woman he had married not out of love, but obligation. While she worked tirelessly to hold their family together, he sought solace in the excitement and validation he found outside their home. In his mind, he had earned it. He had sacrificed his youth, his dreams, and his freedom—was it so wrong to seek comfort with someone who saw him as the brilliant man he wanted to be, rather than the reluctant husband he had become?

When his wife discovered the truth, it shattered what little trust remained. For her, it wasn't just the betrayal of his infidelity—it was the confirmation of a truth she had long suspected: that she was never the woman he truly wanted, and that their life together had been built on a foundation of duty rather than love.

The divorce was bitter, though Russell Jr., ever the pragmatist, tried to frame it as inevitable. In public, he maintained his polished image, spinning the narrative to protect his reputation. Privately, however, the fallout was far more damaging. His wife left with their son, severing ties with the family he had once tried to provide for.

Russell Sr. firmly insisted that Russell Jr. annul his marriage to Frances, convinced that once his son completed college, Frances would lay claim to his financial resources. Faced with the threat of losing his father's financial support, Russell Jr. reluctantly complied, struggling under the weight of his father's control. Frances, left with no choice, was forced to accept the annulment; despite the emotional toll it took on both of them.

After the annulment, Russell Jr. buried himself even deeper in his studies, using his growing success to mask the void left by his failed marriage. Yet, the stain of his infidelity lingered, slowly reshaping how others viewed him.

Frances, on the other hand, had little recourse. As a young Black woman in the early 1950s, challenging the annulment would have been nearly impossible, especially without financial or familial support. She was left to pick up the pieces of a relationship that had been stripped from her—one that, in the eyes of the law and society, had never officially existed.

The ink on his annulment papers had barely dried when Russell Jr. met Barbara Ann. She was unlike any woman he had ever known. Educated, sophisticated, and exuding a quiet confidence, Barbara Ann stood in stark contrast to the girl he had been forced to marry at 18. She represented everything he had always desired: elegance, independence, and a partnership rooted in choice rather than obligation.

Their courtship was swift but calculated. Barbara Ann, with her sharp intellect, was as drawn to Russell Jr.'s charm and ambition as he was to her grace and refinement. To the outside world, they seemed like the perfect match—a power couple destined for greatness.

By the time they married in a small but glamorous ceremony, Russell Jr.'s career was on an upward trajectory. Barbara Ann, with her poise and social connections, became not just his wife but also his partner in building the life he envisioned. Together, they projected an image of success: a shining example of Black excellence in an era still defined by systemic barriers.

Over the years that followed, Barbara Ann gave birth to three beautiful children, and their home became a reflection of their carefully curated lives. Russell Jr., ever the provider, ensured his family lived in comfort and style at their home in Baltimore County.

But beneath the surface, cracks began to form.

For all her sophistication, Barbara Ann was no stranger to the whispers that followed her husband. She had heard about his reputation, his affairs, and his relentless need for validation. She tolerated much of it—believing in the image of their family, if not always the reality. Still, she demanded a level of respect and accountability that Russell Jr. wasn't accustomed to. Unlike his first wife, Barbara Ann was not content to quietly endure his indiscretions.

Their marriage became a dance of appearances and compromises, love and resentment. Russell Jr. adored Barbara Ann's elegance and intelligence, but he struggled with the constraints of fidelity and the pressures of balancing family life against his ambition. For her part, Barbara Ann often felt like she was managing not just her children but her husband's ego.

Despite the challenges, Barbara Ann's influence on Russell Jr. was undeniable. She brought stability to his otherwise chaotic world, grounding him in moments when his ambition threatened to consume him. But as his career reached its peak and his darker impulses began to surface, even Barbara Ann's steady hand couldn't keep him from spiraling toward his eventual downfall.

Meanwhile, Russell Jr. also had to juggle his emotions regarding his father's new marriage and growing family. It sparked a mix of resentment and renewed struggles with his own identity. Having always felt the pressure of living up to his father's expectations, the idea of Russell Sr. starting over with a younger wife, Evelyn Farmer, felt like a personal rejection. It deepened the wounds from his annulled marriage to Frances, reinforcing the belief that his father had always exerted control over his life while pursuing his own happiness without regard for his son's.

Evelyn, being much younger, brought an entirely different energy into the Carrington household. She was ambitious in her own way, perhaps even viewing her marriage as a strategic move. With the prospect of new children, Russell Jr. worried about his place in the family and whether his father would divert financial and emotional support to this new household, further alienating him.

As Russell Sr. settled into his marriage with Evelyn and started a family, the strain between him and Russell Jr. deepened. Russell Jr. saw his father lavishing attention on his young wife and, eventually, their newborn children—something he had never experienced as a son. He watched as the once rigid and controlling figure in his life grew more relaxed, even indulgent, with his new family. This only fueled a sense of bitterness, reinforcing the idea that he had been molded simply as an heir rather than loved as a child.

At family gatherings, the tension was palpable. Evelyn, keenly aware of the friction, tried to play the role of peacemaker, but her presence alone was enough to ignite Russell Jr.'s resentment. He viewed her as a usurper, someone who had taken the little emotional space he once occupied in his father's life. Worse, Evelyn—while polite—was not naïve. She understood that her position as Russell Sr.'s wife secured her future, and she subtly asserted herself in family matters, much to Genevieve's silent dismay.

The breaking point came when Russell Sr. announced plans to revise his Will to include his new children. Russell Jr., already grappling with his own struggles for identity and autonomy, felt as though he was being erased. Fearing his father would prioritize his new family over him, he confronted Russell Sr. one evening. After a particularly tense exchange, Russell Jr. bluntly asked whether his father had ever truly seen him as a son—or merely an investment.

Russell Sr., unshaken, reminded him that everything he possessed now—the prestige, the education, the career—was because of his father's influence. But Russell Jr. no longer saw it that way. He began to question whether his success was truly his own or just another extension of his father's control.

Chapter 3

Morgan's Promise

Russell Jr.'s time at Morgan State College was transformative. The historically Black institution was more than a place of learning; it was also a hub of activism and ambition. At Morgan, he found himself among peers who, like him, were determined to break barriers and redefine their futures in a segregated society.

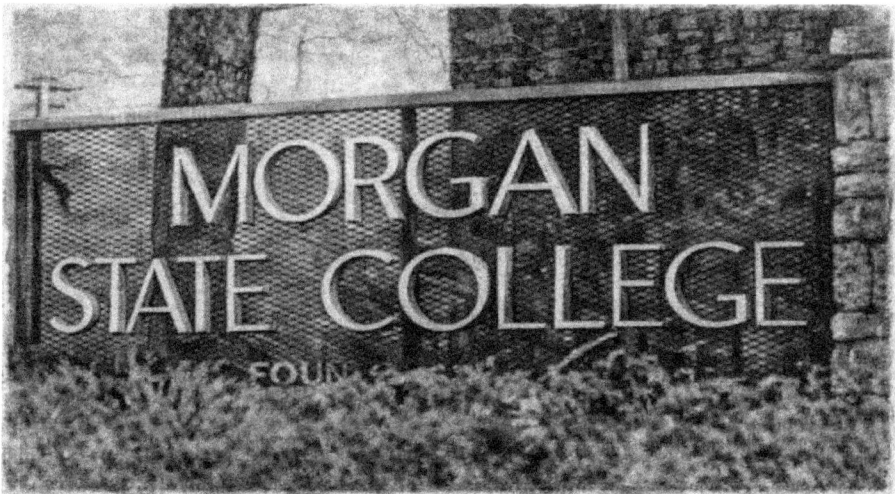

Morgan State College in the early 1950s was a microcosm of the larger struggle for civil rights, shaping Russell Jr. in ways he hadn't anticipated. The campus, filled with passionate students and professors, was a place where ideas collided and new dreams took root. For Russell Jr., it was an awakening. He saw the potential not only for personal success but also for contributing to the fight for equality and social justice. Though Morgan State was a haven for Black students during a time when their opportunities were often limited, it was also a place where students were encouraged to think critically and push against societal norms.

Russell Jr. had always been driven by a desire to prove himself, but his time at Morgan ignited a fire within him. He joined several student organizations and became involved in campus discussions about race and the role of education in shaping a better future for African Americans. He was no longer just a boy from West Baltimore trying to outrun the shadows of being Black—he was a young man on a mission to make a lasting impact.

As Russell Jr. and Donald strolled across the Morgan State footbridge, the clatter of their dress shoes echoed against the steel. It was a daily ritual, their conversations shifting from childhood dreams to the fast-moving reality of college life. Below them, Herring Run trickled lazily; students dotting across the grass, and the campus buzzed with the energy of a new school year.

Donald adjusted the strap of his bookbag.

"So, what you thinking? Alpha or Kappa?"

Russell Jr. smirked. "Man, my father's been pushing Alpha since before I could walk. You already know how that conversation's gonna go."

Donald chuckled. "Yeah, but what you want? You trying to follow in his footsteps, or you gonna do your own thing?"

Russell Jr. sighed, glancing toward the student union where a group of sharply dressed young men stood, laughing and shaking hands.

"I don't know yet. My father—he sees everything like a move on a chessboard. He thinks joining Alpha is about connections, legacy, and the right kind of respect."

Donald nodded. "Can't say he's wrong. But man, this is our time. We ain't just kids in West Baltimore anymore. We got choices." He grinned. "Like whether we're hitting that Omega party Friday night."

Russell Jr. laughed, shaking his head. "You don't miss a beat, do you?"

"Hell no," Donald said, flashing his trademark grin. "College ain't just about books. You gotta live a little. Make some memories before you're stuck in a clinic pulling teeth all day."

Russell Jr. chuckled but fell quiet for a moment. He knew Donald was right—college was a fresh start, a chance to carve out his own identity. But the weight of his father's expectations, his marriage, and his own ambitions loomed over him like storm clouds.

As they reached the other side of the bridge, Donald nudged him. "Just promise me one thing—don't think too hard. Sometimes you just gotta go with what feels right."

Russell Jr. exhaled, nodding. "Yeah. You might be onto something, Donald."

They stepped off the bridge and onto the next chapter of their journey, the path ahead still uncertain but filled with possibility.

Despite the challenges of attending an underfunded institution, Russell Jr. excelled academically. He was known for his sharp mind and quiet determination. His professors—many of whom were leaders in the African American community—took a special interest in him. They recognized his potential and encouraged him to pursue dentistry, not just for personal gain but as a way to uplift his community.

"If you can heal the body, you can heal the spirit," one of his mentors told him during his sophomore year. Those words stayed with Russell Jr. throughout his career, shaping his approach to both his profession and his life.

Though he faced obstacles in a segregated society, Russell Jr's resolve never wavered. At Morgan, he found camaraderie in a group of ambitious students who shared his belief that they could achieve greatness despite the odds. They were the children of the Harlem

Renaissance, inspired by the trailblazers who had fought for Black dignity in a hostile world. Russell Jr. became part of this wave— determined to carve out his own space in a world that often told him he didn't belong.

One of the most pivotal moments during his time at Morgan occurred when a local physician, who had previously been a guest lecturer at the college, invited him to shadow at the Black-owned and operated Provident Hospital. Dr. James O'Neil, a successful Black physician who had defied racial expectations, was a teaching dean at the only Black hospital in the heart of Baltimore. For Russell Jr., it was a glimpse into the future he had always dreamed of.

Under Dr. O'Neil's mentorship, he learned that medical practice was not just a means of livelihood—it was a way to empower the Black community, offering a service that was both vital and often overlooked.

By the time he graduated from Morgan in 1954, Russell Jr. had developed a deep understanding of the social and political dynamics that shaped his path. He had witnessed firsthand the challenges that Black physicians faced, but he was undeterred. He knew that, if given the opportunity, he could become a leader in his field. Morgan State College had equipped him not only with the technical skills to excel in life but also with the intellectual tools to challenge the status quo.

After earning his Bachelor's degree in Psychology, Russell Jr. faced a new set of challenges as he set his sights on medical school. The journey ahead was daunting for any young Black man, but for someone like Russell Jr.—eager to prove himself yet acutely aware of the hurdles that came with his race—it was especially formidable. In the mid-1950s, many medical and dental schools were only just beginning to desegregate, and the transition was far from seamless.

Russell Jr. applied to several prestigious dental schools, but each rejection letter, though couched in professional language, carried an unspoken message: his race was a determining factor. Schools in the North were somewhat more open to integrating Black students, but even in those institutions, Black students faced open hostility, subtle discrimination, and an isolating sense of exclusion that could be crushing.

After months of waiting, Russell Jr. was finally accepted to the newly integrated University of Kansas City Medical College. It wasn't an Ivy League school, but it held a strong reputation, and for Russell Jr., the acceptance felt like a victory.

Russell Jr. and Donald sat on the worn leather couch in Donald's small apartment just off campus, a stack of rejection letters spread across the coffee table like discarded playing cards. The air smelled of old books and the faint trace of Donald's last cup of coffee, long gone cold.

"Man," Donald sighed, rubbing his temples. "Kansas was my last hope. I thought for sure I had a shot there."

Russell Jr. leaned forward, flipping through the letters: Howard. Meharry. Kansas. All no. He shook his head. "They don't know what they're passing up."

Donald exhaled sharply, leaning back against the couch. "I was ready to follow your lead, you know? Dental school. At least we'd be in it together. But now?" He gestured toward the letters. "Feels like I'm out of moves."

A knock at the door interrupted them. Donald stood, stretching before swinging it open to reveal an unexpected guest—Mr. **Thurgood Marshall.**

"Donald," Marshall greeted, stepping inside with his usual commanding presence. "Russell." He nodded in acknowledgment.

Russell Jr. stood, shaking his hand. He had met Mr. Marshall several times with his father, Russell Sr. Thurgood Marshall—the civil rights attorney making waves across the country—was a longtime friend of Donald's family.

Mr. Marshall didn't waste time. "I hear you're thinking about giving up."

Donald sighed. "Not much of a choice, Mr. Marshall. Every school I applied to turned me down."

Marshall smirked, shaking his head. "That's because you were looking in the wrong places." He pulled out an envelope and handed it to Donald. "You're going to apply here."

Donald read the letterhead aloud. "University of Maryland School of Medicine?" He frowned. "They've never accepted us."

Mr. Marshall crossed his arms. "That's why you're going to be the first." His tone was firm, unwavering. "You have the grades, the qualifications—everything they claim they look for. And if they try to deny you because of the color of your skin, well..." His smirk returned. "They'll have to answer to me."

Russell and Donald exchanged glances.

Donald exhaled, shaking his head. "You really think they'll take me?"

"I know they will," Mr. Marshall said. "And if they don't, I'll make sure they explain why—in front of a judge."

A slow smile spread across Donald's face. For the first time in weeks, something that had felt impossible now seemed within reach.

Russell Jr. patted his friend on the back. "Looks like you won't be pulling teeth with me after all."

Donald chuckled. "Nah, man. But you'll still be my first call when I need a good dentist."

They laughed, the weight of rejection lifting just a little. With Mr.

Marshall in his corner, Donald wasn't just applying to medical school—he was making history.

The moment Russell Jr. arrived at the University of Kansas, the challenges became immediately apparent. While the administration was technically welcoming, many faculty members and students were less than pleased to have a Black student among them. Russell Jr. had heard the stories—of Black students being subjected to higher scrutiny, assigned to less desirable clinical shifts, and given disproportionate workloads to prove themselves. What he hadn't anticipated was the emotional toll these challenges would take on him.

In the early days, he faced ridicule from classmates who whispered behind his back, refused to work with him on group projects, or outright excluded him from conversations. In lecture halls, he was often the only Black face in the room, and the unspoken tension was palpable. Faculty members, while professional on the surface, would frequently avoid eye contact, rarely acknowledging his potential. One professor, in particular, seemed determined to make Russell Jr.'s life more difficult. He regularly assigned him the most complex cases in the clinic, forcing him to work longer hours while other students breezed through.

Despite the isolation, Russell Jr.'s resolve remained unshaken. He threw himself into his studies, often staying late into the night in the school's library, determined to prove that he belonged. The discrimination only fueled his drive to excel. He refused to give anyone the satisfaction of seeing him fail. And as his knowledge grew, so did his confidence.

During his first year, he earned a reputation as a diligent student and a skilled practitioner. The work was grueling, but he had the discipline to persevere. Slowly, his classmates began to see him in a different light. They came to realize that Russell Jr. wasn't there because of a token acceptance—he was there because he was as capable and as committed as any other student.

But just as Russell Jr. began to gain some respect, the real challenge emerged: navigating the institutionalized racism that still permeated the medical and dental fields. He was often denied internships or placements at high-profile clinics, as many practitioners in the field were hesitant to work with a Black student—even one who had proven his competence. This was a reality he hadn't anticipated. He had assumed that earning a degree and excelling in his studies would open doors for him. But in a world where Black professionals were still rare and often regarded with suspicion, even the most well-earned credentials didn't guarantee acceptance.

With renewed determination, Russell Jr. completed medical school and went on to earn both a Master's degree and a PhD from the University of Kansas. He later received his Doctor of Dental Surgery (DDS) degree from Western Reserve University in Cleveland, Ohio— becoming one of the few Black men to earn a dental degree at a time when many white professionals still resisted the inclusion of Black colleagues in their ranks.

His breakthrough came when he secured an internship in the Department of Oral Surgery at Provident Hospital in his hometown of Baltimore.

Provident Hospital in Baltimore holds a significant place in history as one of the first medical facilities founded by and for African Americans. Established in 1894 by a group of Black physicians, including Dr. Nathan Francis Mossell, its mission was to provide quality medical care to Black patients at a time when segregation barred them from treatment in most hospitals. It also served as a critical training ground for Black nurses and doctors, offering opportunities otherwise denied in predominantly white institutions.

The hospital's legacy loomed large in his community, standing defiantly in the face of systemic exclusion. As a young boy, Russell Jr.—later known as Dr. Carrington—marveled at the tales of pioneering physicians who had built Provident from the ground up, daring to create a space where others refused.

By the time Russell Jr. was accepted into medical school, Provident Hospital had become more than a beacon; it was a symbol of possibility. His internship there introduced him to a world of Black excellence in medicine, where doctors and nurses worked tirelessly—not only to save lives but also to prove their worth in a society that continually underestimated them. For Dr. Carrington, Provident wasn't just a hospital; it was a proving ground, a place where he honed his skills and cultivated his vision of what the future of oral dentistry could hold.

Dr. Carrington was acutely aware of the limitations imposed by the broader medical community. He dreamed of a career that transcended Provident Hospital, one that would position him not just as a Black doctor but also as a leader in cutting-edge dental practices. This dream became a driving force in his career.

As his ambition propelled him into the upper echelons of medicine, the lessons of Provident never left him. Its halls reminded him of his roots and the sacrifices made by those who came before him. It was there that he first donned his signature white coat, his perfect smile masking the insecurities and internal conflicts that would later haunt him.

When Dr. Carrington left Provident Hospital, stepping into a world where the stakes were higher and the scrutiny harsher, the lessons he learned stayed with him—but so did the burden of representation. Every success he achieved was seen as a victory not just for himself but for the entire Black community. By the mid-1960s, Dr. Russell Carrington Jr.'s career had skyrocketed. Invitations to conferences, guest lectures, and panels poured in, giving him countless opportunities to showcase his brilliance on a national stage.

Chapter 4

Cracks Beneath the Veneer

At first, the travel and lectures offered Dr. Carrington an escape—a reprieve from the weight of his growing practice and the unrelenting expectations he had placed on himself. Each city was a fresh start, an opportunity to bask in the admiration of his peers and the adoration of audiences eager to learn from the man hailed as a pioneer in his field. But as the months turned into years, the lines began to blur. The devoted family man and esteemed professional slowly gave way to someone far more indulgent, far less disciplined.

Dr. Carrington's charm, once an asset in the office and lecture halls, began to take on a life of its own. He relished the attention, and soon whispers about his exploits followed him wherever he went. Colleagues at conferences turned knowing glances into hushed conversations, and the women who lingered too long after his lectures only added to the burgeoning myth of Dr. Carrington, the playboy dentist.

His reputation grew faster than his practice. Some women drove hours just for a fleeting lunch with him, their cars pulling up outside his office with Washington, D.C., license plates gleaming in the midday sun. Russell Sr., ever the watchful father, couldn't help but notice. One afternoon, he sat silently, his eyes fixed on the steady parade of cars coming and going from the office parking lot. The women left with flustered smiles, their laughter lingering in the air long after they were gone.

"It's just lunch, Pop," Russell Jr. said with a dismissive wave when his father broached the subject. "You know how people are—they love a little charm."

But Russell Sr. saw more than charm; he saw the cracks forming beneath the polished veneer. He saw the son he had raised teetering on the edge of excess, pulled by the allure of a life far removed from the values he and Genevieve had tried to instill.

"Russell," his father said quietly, his voice weighted with concern, "a man can lose himself quicker than he thinks. Don't mistake their attention for respect, and don't let it turn you into someone you're not."

But the warning fell on deaf ears. The applause, the admiration, the fleeting encounters—they filled a void that Dr. Carrington couldn't quite name. Each indulgence was a distraction, a momentary high that made it easier to ignore the fractures deepening in his carefully constructed life.

Things worsened when Barbara Ann arrived early for her regularly scheduled hair appointment. The whispers had finally reached her ears. Her heart pounded as she sat frozen under the dryer, pretending to read *Jet* magazine, though the words blurred before her eyes. The women around her spoke in hushed tones, but there was no mistaking the subject.

"Chile", you know Frances' boy looks just like Dr. Carrington." "Mmm-hmm. Spitting image. He come by here all the time, playing while she do hair."

"Aint no way Barbara Ann don't know. She got to know by now."

Barbara Ann clenched her fists in her lap, pressing her nails into her palms. She wanted to turn around and demand they say it to her face—but she didn't. Instead, she let the hum of the dryer drown out their voices.

She left the shop without saying a word, her polished heels clicking against the pavement. The late-afternoon sun burned against her skin, but inside, she felt cold. She had suspected something—late nights at the office, vague answers when she asked about his past—but she had never imagined this.

That evening, as Dr. Carrington walked through the door, hanging his coat with his usual precision, Barbara Ann stood in the middle of the living room, arms crossed.

"Russell," she said, her voice steady but sharp. "Who is Russell the Third?"

He froze, his hand still gripping the hanger. The weight of his secret bore down on him. He had always been so careful. But Baltimore wasn't a city for secrets—not with all those beauty shop conversations and church pew whispers.

His mouth opened, then closed. For the first time in his life, Dr. Russell Carrington Jr. had no answer.

The silence between them stretched, thick and suffocating. Barbara Ann's eyes never left his face, searching for some flicker of remorse, an explanation—anything.

"You heard me," she said, stepping forward. "Who is Russell the Third?"

Dr. Carrington exhaled slowly, gathering himself. He had spent years perfecting the art of control—his words, his image, his reputation—but standing before Barbara Ann now, he realized he had no control over this moment.

"He's my son," he finally admitted, his voice quieter than she expected.

Barbara Ann's breath hitched, but she willed herself not to react. "And Frances?"

Russell hesitated. "I was married to her—briefly. It was annulled."

A bitter laugh escaped Barbara Ann's lips before she could stop it. "Annulled? So you thought that erased it? That made it disappear?" She shook her head. "My God, Russell… how long were you going to keep this from me?"

"I was protecting you," he said, stepping closer. "Protecting *us*. It was over before you and I ever—"

"Don't you dare," she cut him off, her voice trembling now. "Don't you *dare* act like this was nothing. A whole child, Russell. A whole child, right here in this city, with people talking about it in my presence like I'm the fool."

Russell closed his eyes, rubbing his temple. He knew he had underestimated Baltimore—a city where everybody knew somebody. He had convinced himself that by keeping quiet, by pushing Frances and Russell III to the periphery of his life, he could rewrite his own story without consequence. But the past wasn't so easily buried.

"I was going to tell you," he said, though even to his own ears, the words felt hollow.

"When?" Barbara Ann demanded. "When he was grown? When some stranger told me instead? Or were you just hoping I'd never find out?"

Russell had no answer.

Barbara Ann inhaled deeply, steadying herself. "I need some air." She grabbed her purse and walked past him, leaving the door swinging open in her wake.

Dr. Carrington stood in the center of their immaculate home, the silence pressing down heavier than any accusation. For the first time, he realized he might not be able to talk his way out of this.

Later that night, Barbara Ann gripped the phone tightly, pacing the length of the kitchen as she waited for an answer. Finally, Dr. Carrington's stepsister, Joyce, sighed on the other end. "Hello."

"Why didn't you tell me?" Barbara Ann demanded, her voice sharp with betrayal.

"What did you expect?" Joyce shot back. "My father and brother would kill me if I got in the middle of Russell's business. And besides, Frances ain't checking for my brother no more. She moved on."

Barbara Ann scoffed. "Moved on? You mean she *moved on* with their son? The one I just found out about yesterday?"

Joyce hesitated. "Listen, Barbara Ann, I didn't keep it from you to be cruel. I just knew it wasn't my place. And truth be told, I figured you'd find out eventually. Baltimore's too small for secrets."

Barbara Ann ran a hand over her forehead, the weight of it all settling deep in her bones. She had trusted Joyce. Over the years, she had come to see her as family—someone who could level with her about Dr. Carrington's ways.

"And what about you?" Barbara Ann asked. "What do *you* think about all this?"

Joyce sighed again. "I think my brother is who he's always been—a man who hates losing control. And you, Barbara Ann? You're learning the hard way that Russell only tells the truth when he has no choice."

Barbara Ann's stomach twisted. She knew Joyce was right. But now that the truth was out, the real question remained—what was she going to do about it?

Joyce hesitated before continuing, her voice dropping lower. "I've seen the boy a few times. He's a Carrington through and through—same eyes, same damn walk. You wouldn't need a blood test to know he's Russell's son."

Barbara Ann's grip tightened around the phone. "I don't want Russell near him or Frances. And he better not be giving them a dime."

Joyce sighed. "Barbara, you think you can control that man? Russell does what Russell wants. But no, far as I know, he's kept his distance.

He ain't exactly a doting father."

Barbara Ann exhaled sharply, trying to steady her emotions. "Good. He built this life with me, and I'll be damned if I let some woman from his past come knocking at my door."

"You think Frances wants him back?" Joyce asked, almost amused. "That woman's got her own life. She ain't chasing Russell."

"I don't care what she wants," Barbara Ann snapped. "I care about what's *mine*."

Joyce went quiet for a moment before speaking again. "You sure you're mad at Frances? Or are you mad at Russell?"

Barbara Ann swallowed hard. She didn't have an answer for that.

PART 2

Chapter 5

Dreams in White Coats

In the early years of his private practice at 3414 Duvall Avenue, Dr. Carrington's charm and surgical skill drew patients from all walks of life. His reputation grew rapidly, and he soon became a sought-after figure—one of the few Black doctors breaking into exclusive medical circles that had long been closed to people like him. He was even on staff at Rosewood State Hospital in Owings Mills, Maryland, after the hospital was integrated and African American patients were transferred there. Yet, as his fame spread, so did whispers of his arrogance and ambition.

By the late 1960s, Dr. Russell Carrington Jr., a rising dental surgeon, and Dr. Donald Stewart, a respected pediatrician, had solidified their places among Baltimore's Black elite. Their journey—from two boys walking the cracked sidewalks of West Baltimore, dreaming of escape, to becoming doctors featured in *Jet* Magazine—was a testament to their resilience, ambition, and the power of perseverance.

At a swanky gala at Baltimore's Famous Ballroom, the two men stood side by side, dressed in tailored suits, sipping bourbon as they mingled with other Black professionals—lawyers, politicians, business owners, and educators. The event was a fundraiser for a local scholarship fund, the kind of affair that symbolized their arrival into a world they had once only dreamed about.

Dr. Stewart smirked, holding up a copy of *Jet* Magazine that featured both their names in an article titled *Baltimore's Finest: Dr. Russell Carrington Jr. and Dr. Donald Stewart Give Back to Their Community.*

"Man, would you look at that?" Dr. Stewart said, nudging Dr. Carrington. "Two kids from West Baltimore, now in *Jet* like we're somebody."

Dr. Carrington chuckled, shaking his head as he took the magazine. The article highlighted their contributions to the Black community— Dr. Carrington for his work in advancing dental surgery techniques and providing affordable care to underserved families, and Dr. Stewart for his tireless efforts in pediatric medicine, advocating for better healthcare access for Black children.

"We *are* somebody," Dr. Carrington said, flipping through the pages.

"But you know, my father would probably say this is just a publicity stunt. 'Respect isn't in print, it's in power,'" he mimicked in a deep, authoritative tone.

Dell laughed. "Man, your old man was always about strategy. But this?" He tapped the magazine. "This means something. Representation matters."

Russell nodded, scanning the room filled with successful Black professionals, each carving their own path despite the obstacles. "You're right. We've come a long way."

Dr. Stewart raised his glass. "To making it."

Dr. Carrington clinked his glass against his. "And to what's next."

As the night continued, they basked in their success, fully aware that their journey wasn't just their own. They were proof that Black excellence in Baltimore wasn't just possible—it was inevitable.

Later, Dr. Carrington went on to receive a major citation for his contribution to Dentistry and Allied Sciences from the United States Army Registry of Clinical Oral Pathology at Walter Reed Army Hospital in Washington, D.C. The award was presented to select members of the medical field and its allied sciences for contributions involving outstanding and rare cases in their respective fields.

Dr. Carrington reported on a relatively uncommon tumor diagnosed as a *Fibro adenoma Blastoma*, which he discovered in the mouth and nasal area of a six-year-old child. To date, this type of tumor had not been previously reported in this age group. The case was permanently accessioned at the United States Army Registry of Clinical Oral Pathology at Walter Reed Army Hospital.

Collaborating on the surgery with Dr. Carrington was Dr. Martin Rodney of Provident Hospital's dental staff. The surgical team successfully removed the giant tumor from the roof of the child's mouth, restoring the face to its normal contour.

Dr. Carrington soon began accepting invitations to exclusive clubs and high-profile dinners, where his presence was as much a political statement as it was a professional acknowledgment. He became a respected member of the Baltimore City and Maryland Dental Society. Russell's magnetic personality could disarm even the most prejudiced of gatekeepers. That same smile that had once symbolized hope and confidence now became his armor.

Provident had once been a place of unity, where Black professionals stood together against a common enemy. But in his new world, Russell's relentless pursuit of perfection left no room for mistakes. The pressure of maintaining his flawless, capable, and untouchable image began to take its toll. Behind the polished façade, Russell harbored desires that could jeopardize everything he had built. What once felt like an unstoppable rise now seemed precarious—each step forward bringing him closer to a fall he couldn't escape.

Dr. Carrington's influence continued to grow, bolstered by his financial contributions to public causes, including significant efforts like the Provident Hospital Development Program. His generosity and leadership earned him the role of head of the Small Business Division of community outreach, a position that cemented his role as both a medical and civic leader.

In 1960, Russell and a group of ambitious young Black physicians set out to apply the medical business model they had learned from the experienced doctors at Provident. Their goal was to build and open another Black-owned medical facility in West Baltimore. To achieve this, they partnered to form a real estate development company called Del Enterprises, Inc., led by Russell's good friend Dr. Donald W. Stewart—another brilliant and visionary young Black doctor in his own right.

In 1966, Dr. Russell Carrington Jr.'s innovative vision was recognized when he secured an $83,000 grant from the U.S. Public Health Service. This grant not only underscored his brilliance but also solidified his standing in the medical field. With these funds, Dr. Carrington had the resources to push the boundaries of his research, expand his practice, and develop groundbreaking programs that would become a cornerstone for combating childhood tooth decay.

Dr. Carrington was instrumental in introducing oral healthcare to preschool children from low-income families through the *Head Start* program. Launched in the summer of 1965, *Head Start* aimed to provide comprehensive early childhood services, and Dr. Carrington leveraged his relationship with Baltimore Public Schools to gain access to local inner-city schools. His partnership allowed him to establish a pioneering model for delivering preventive dental care and education directly to young children in underserved communities.

By working closely with educators and administrators, Dr. Carrington ensured that oral healthcare became an integral part of the school environment. His efforts not only improved the immediate health outcomes of these children but also laid the groundwork for long-term awareness about dental hygiene among families in Baltimore.

One of the unique challenges he faced was overcoming the stigma and fear surrounding dental care, particularly in communities with limited prior access to such services. To address this, he made dental visits approachable and engaging for young children. He collaborated with teachers and administrators to incorporate dental health education into the curriculum, using creative methods like storytelling and interactive demonstrations to make learning fun and memorable.

His efforts during the early 1970s became a beacon of progress in a time of heightened social awareness and reform. The program not only transformed the lives of the children it directly served but also sparked a broader conversation about the importance of preventive healthcare in the Black community. His work was a microcosm of the growing recognition in the 1970s of the interconnectedness of education, healthcare, and poverty alleviation.

Ultimately, his work gained recognition from local and national organizations, further cementing his reputation as a pioneer in public health. For Dr. Carrington, however, the true reward came from seeing the confidence and smiles of the children whose lives he helped change.

But one child he neglected along this journey was his own.

Frances was no fool. She knew Dr. Carrington could dodge phone calls, ignore letters, and pretend Russell III didn't exist in his day-to-day life, but there was one thing he couldn't ignore: his profession.

So she played the only card she had. Every six months, like clockwork, she scheduled Russell III's dental appointments at Dr. Carrington's office. Not at some other clinic. Not with a colleague. At *his* office.

The first time, Dr. Carrington barely looked at his son. He kept it clinical, asking routine questions and avoiding eye contact. Frances sat in the exam room, arms crossed, watching every move. If he wanted to act like this child wasn't his, she would remind him in the most deliberate way possible.

"Open your mouth," he muttered, inspecting Russell III's teeth.

Russell III did as he was told, his dark eyes—Carrington eyes—searching his father's face, waiting for a recognition that never came.

"He's got strong teeth," Dr. Carrington said stiffly to Frances after the appointment.

"Of course he does," she shot back. "He's yours."

This went on for years. Each appointment was a reminder—a confrontation without words. Frances never asked for money. She never demanded his time. She only ensured that at least twice a year, Dr. Carrington had to face the son he was neglecting.

And maybe, just maybe, one day he'd see more than just a set of teeth.

Maybe he'd finally see his son.

Chapter 6

Charm and Consequences

A private meeting room at the Lord Baltimore Hotel. Sunlight filters through tall windows, casting long shadows over a polished mahogany table. Dr. Russell Carrington Jr. sits impeccably dressed, exuding confidence, his disarming smile masking his true intent. Across the table sits James Rouse, the visionary developer responsible for reshaping Baltimore's landscape.

Dr. Carrington opens the conversation with subtle flattery, praising Rouse's groundbreaking work on projects like Columbia and the Inner Harbor redevelopment. His charm is deliberate but understated, designed to make Rouse feel both respected and intrigued.

"Mr. Rouse, your vision for Baltimore is exactly what this city needs—a future built on unity, progress, and opportunity. You've not just redefined real estate; you've redefined possibility. It's inspiring."

Rouse, a man well accustomed to flattery, leans back in his chair, studying Dr. Carrington with mild amusement.

"Flattery's a good start, Dr. Carrington. But I assume you didn't call this meeting just to boost my ego."

Dr. Carrington chuckles, leaning forward slightly, creating a sense of intimacy.

"You're right, of course. I called this meeting because I believe we share a common goal. We both want to see Baltimore thrive—not just its downtown, but its communities. And that's where my group of physicians comes in."

He unveils his plan: a network of high-quality medical clinics embedded in underserved neighborhoods throughout Baltimore. The clinics, he claims, will provide much-needed care while revitalizing areas that have long been neglected. Beneath this noble proposal lies his real ambition—to acquire undervalued real estate in these neighborhoods, fully aware that Rouse's larger developments will drive up property values.

Rouse is intrigued but cautious. He's no stranger to ambitious men, and he senses there's more to Dr. Carrington's plan than meets the eye.

"Your vision is compelling, Dr. Carrington. But revitalization takes more than medical clinics. What makes you think your plan will succeed?"

Dr. Carrington leans back, his smile widening.

"Because I'm not just building clinics—I'm building trust. I know these communities. I've walked these streets, cared for their families, and earned their

respect. With your support, we can create something lasting—a partnership that transforms lives."

Rouse is almost convinced, but he presses for more assurance. The tension in the room rises as Dr. Carrington carefully deploys every ounce of his charm. His voice softens, his words becoming almost poetic as he paints a vivid picture of a future where their collaboration reshapes Baltimore for generations.

Eventually, Rouse agrees to meet again, charmed by Dr. Carrington's vision and passion.

As Dr. Carrington leaves the meeting, his confident smile fades for just a moment. Beneath his polished exterior lies a man driven not by altruism, but by an insatiable hunger for power and control.

PIONEERS – OF DEL ENTERPRIZES Three Quarters of an Million Dollar Development of Garwyn Medical Center Dedication

In 1969, the charter members of Del Enterprises, Inc. cemented their place among Baltimore's Black elite by opening the first private medical facility financed by Black investors in Baltimore City. The physician-led investment succeeded without needing James Rouse's backing after all.

Garwyn Medical Center, located at 2300 Garrison Boulevard in Baltimore, Maryland, holds a significant place in the city's medical and cultural history. It was a beacon of progress for the Black community—a testament to self-reliance, vision, and determination.

One of Del Enterprises' most infamous acquisitions, however, came from their relationship with Rouse: a luxurious condo in the exclusive Harper House at the Village of Cross Keys. The development symbolized progress and prestige—a once-segregated community transformed into a haven for Baltimore's elite. For Dr. Carrington and his associates, it was more than just an investment. It provided a discreet location for their escapades.

To outsiders, the condo was simply another wise financial move. But for Dr. Carrington, it became a second home—a retreat where he could shed the burdens of his public and private lives. The Harper House address even appeared on his Maryland identification, a subtle nod to the duality of his existence. For those who knew the truth, however, it was something else entirely: a refuge for affairs, late-night parties, and whispered secrets.

The Cross Keys condo blurred professional boundaries and became a place where reputations were quietly gambled. Here, Dr. Carrington indulged in the power and freedom his status afforded him, even as the cost of those indulgences began to mount. His colleagues—many of whom shared his penchant for secrecy—only emboldened him, their collective silence forming a shield against scandal.

But the walls of even the most exclusive communities have ears. Whispers about the condo began to circulate, adding to the growing cloud of suspicion surrounding Dr. Carrington. Eventually, the rumors became so persistent that most people assumed Russell Jr. and Barbara Ann were divorced or legally separated.

Dr. Carrington spared no expense decorating the Cross Keys condo, his private sanctuary tucked away from prying eyes. It was a reflection of his meticulously curated image—sophistication, success, and just a touch of excess. Every detail was carefully considered, crafting a space that both impressed and seduced.

The living room was anchored by an oversized Italian leather sectional, its deep cognac hue complementing the floor-to-ceiling windows that bathed the room in natural light. A Persian rug, handwoven in vibrant reds and golds, sprawled beneath the furniture, grounding the modern aesthetic with a sense of timeless luxury.

Contemporary Black artists that Dr. Carrington had discovered on his travels adorned the walls with bold, abstract pieces. Each had a story he loved to recount to his guests. In one corner, a polished brass-and-glass bar cart gleamed, stocked with top-shelf whiskey, bourbon, and cognac—his personal indulgences and the tools of many a persuasive conversation.

The dining area featured a sleek marble-topped table surrounded by minimalist chrome chairs upholstered in velvet. It was here that Dr. Carrington entertained his most intimate guests—clients, colleagues, and, occasionally, the women who came and went from his life like whispers in the night.

His bedroom was equally impressive—a realm of understated opulence. A custom-made four-poster bed dominated the space, draped in Egyptian cotton sheets with a thread count so high it felt like sleeping on air. The nightstands held crystal lamps, their soft light casting a warm glow on the room's deep navy walls.

Even the smallest details were carefully curated. The bathroom featured a freestanding soaking tub, imported tiles, and a walk-in closet filled with bespoke suits, silk ties, and Italian leather shoes—all arranged with the precision of a man who knew that appearance was everything.

The Cross Keys condo wasn't just a home; it was a stage, carefully set for the performance of Dr. Russell Carrington Jr. life style.

The center was one of three African American medical centers established in Baltimore in 1968, with Garwyn Medical Center being the first. Even Governor Marvin Mandel attended the opening ceremony. This medical center offered essential healthcare services to the local community and created professional opportunities for Black medical practitioners at a time when such prospects were limited due to systemic discrimination.

Today, Garwyn Medical Center continues to serve the Baltimore community, hosting a range of medical practices, including podiatry services. The center stands as a testament to the enduring legacy of African American medical professionals in the city.

Chapter 7

The Perfect Smile

It was supposed to be just another lecture. Dr. Russell Carrington Jr. had grown accustomed to standing before captivated audiences, his commanding presence and polished rhetoric leaving little room for anything less than admiration. But on that warm evening at a small historically Black college in Chester, South Carolina, called Brainerd Institute, fate had other plans.

As the crowd thinned and Dr. Carrington prepared to leave, a young woman approached him. She was striking—a 5'3", caramel-complexioned woman with shoulder-length black hair. Her quiet confidence caught him off guard.

"Dr. Carrington," she said, her soft, melodic Southern accent wrapping around each word, "I just had to tell you—you have the most perfect smile I've ever seen."

Her name was Johnnie Mae Warren, and though only 22, her poise and charm commanded his attention. She was single, fresh out of secretary classes, and caring for a young daughter at home. What began as a casual compliment quickly turned into a deep conversation about the migration of Black families from the South to cities like Baltimore, Maryland.

Johnnie Mae shared her own story. Her sister Marjorie had already moved to Baltimore and had been encouraging her to join her. "It might be a task," she admitted with a small laugh, "having a little one to think about and all." Still, her tone carried a note of curiosity, as if she were already imagining the possibilities.

She added, "My sister already got a job at Garwyn Medical Center as a receptionist for another doctor in your building."

Dr. Carrington, ever the opportunist, saw something in Johnnie Mae— a spark of ambition and vulnerability that intrigued him. She was different from the women in his usual social circles back home— unpolished, yes, but refreshingly genuine. He found himself drawn to her, not just for her beauty but for her story. Her struggles, resilience, and dreams reminded him of his own youth, before success consumed him.

Before the evening ended, Dr. Carrington made sure to leave an impression. He gave her his contact information, encouraging her to reach out if she ever decided to move to Baltimore. "It's a city of opportunities," he said, flashing the smile she'd complimented earlier. "You and your daughter could do well there."

As he returned to Baltimore, Dr. Carrington couldn't stop thinking about the chance meeting. It was a dangerous distraction, one he knew could complicate his already precarious personal life. But for a man who had built his life on balancing appearances and indulgences, the allure of Johnnie Mae Warren was too tempting to ignore.

Over the next few weeks, Dr. Carrington found himself replaying their conversation in his mind—her voice, her laugh, and the way she seemed genuinely interested in him, not as a doctor or a public figure, but as a man. She wasn't just another pretty face. There was something about her vulnerability and her hope for a better future that stirred something deep within him.

Dr. Russell Carrington Jr. leaned back in the leather chair of his private dental office, a rare grin playing at his lips as he swirled a glass of brandy in his hand. Across from him, Dr. Donald Stewart sat with his feet propped up on the mahogany desk, already sensing where the conversation was headed.

"I met someone," Dr. Carrington said, taking a slow sip of his drink.

Dr. Stewart arched an eyebrow, amusement flickering across his face.

"Oh yeah? And where exactly did you meet someone this time?"

Dr. Carrington smirked. "At my lecture down in South Carolina—a medical symposium at Brainerd Institute." He paused for effect. "Her name's Johnnie Mae. Smart, ambitious, beautiful."

Dr. Stewart let out a hearty laugh, shaking his head. "Russ, come on, man. You do remember that you're still married, right?"

Russell exhaled, setting his glass down. "It's not like that, Donald. She's different. We talked for hours after the lecture. She understands me."

Dr. Stewart chuckled, sitting up straight. "Understands you, huh? That's what we're calling it now?"

Dr. Carrington rolled his eyes. "I'm serious. She's not just some—" He stopped himself, choosing his words carefully. "She makes me feel…like I don't have to be Dr. Carrington all the time."

Dr. Stewart shook his head, still smirking. "Man, you kill me. You got a whole wife—Barbara Ann, the mother of your kids—at home, and you're out here in South Carolina making connections."

Dr. Carrington sighed, running a hand over his face. "You wouldn't understand."

Dr. Stewart gave him a pointed look. "Oh, I understand just fine. You want to have your cake and eat it too. But let me remind you of something—powerful men don't get the luxury of being sloppy. Your reputation is everything."

Dr. Carrington leaned forward, his expression turning serious. "That's just it, Donald. I'm tired of being the man everyone expects me to be—the perfect husband, the model doctor, the legacy my father sculpted." He shook his head. "Johnnie Mae sees me beyond all that."

Dr. Stewart studied his best friend for a moment before sighing. "You're playing with fire, Russ."

Russell leaned back, picking up his glass again. "Maybe," he admitted. "But for once, I don't care."

Dr. Stewart shook his head, chuckling. "Just don't let Jet Magazine or The Afro catch wind of this."

It didn't take long for him to reach out. At first, it was under the guise of professionalism—a letter expressing his admiration for Johnnie Mae's courage as a young mother, along with an offer to help her settle in Baltimore if she ever decided to make the move. But the tone of his letters quickly became more personal.

Johnnie Mae responded eagerly. She confessed that the idea of moving to Baltimore was becoming more appealing, especially with her sister's encouragement. Her daughter, she wrote, deserved better than what small-town South Carolina could offer. And, truthfully, she admitted that Dr. Carrington's interest in her gave her the courage to consider starting over in a new city.

By the time she decided to relocate, Dr. Carrington had already begun making arrangements. He found her a modest apartment not far from where her sister lived and promised her a job as a receptionist at his office. When she arrived in Baltimore, he was there to greet her, his polished appearance and warm smile reassuring her that she'd made the right choice.

For Johnnie Mae, Dr. Carrington represented stability and a glimpse of the life she had always dreamed of—one filled with sophistication and opportunity. For Dr. Carrington, Johnnie Mae was an escape from the pressures of his marriage to Barbara Ann and the relentless expectations of his public persona.

But as their relationship deepened, it became harder to maintain the illusion of control. Dr. Carrington's colleagues began to notice his frequent absences and whispered about the mysterious young woman he seemed so enamored with. At home, Barbara Ann grew suspicious of his increasing time away, though she chose, for now, to remain silent.

For a while, Dr. Carrington managed to juggle it all: his career, his marriage, and his secret life with Johnnie Mae. Yet it didn't take long for her to sense a subtle shift whenever she accompanied him to his office or attended professional gatherings. At first, the glances from staff and colleagues seemed rooted in admiration or curiosity, but soon the whispers began.

One afternoon, while she was waiting in the reception area, a nurse leaned over and lowered her voice. "You seem sweet, but you ought to know—Dr. Carrington's married. Got kids, too. His wife, Barbara Ann, isn't the type to let things slide. If she ever shows up here or calls, you better act like you don't know anything."

Johnnie Mae froze, the warning hanging in the air. But after the initial sting of shock, she brushed it off. They're just jealous, she thought—jealous of the attention he gives me, jealous of what I have. And what she had was enviable: trips out of town, expensive gifts, and the thrill of riding through Baltimore in his sleek 1971 Mercedes-Benz SL Convertible Roadster.

Dr. Carrington had a way of making her feel special, like she was the only person in the room when he looked at her. He'd reassure her with that perfect smile and his smooth, deliberate charm. "Don't listen to gossip," he'd say, gently stroking her cheek. "People love to talk when they see someone as beautiful as you."

Johnnie Mae wanted to believe him. She told herself that what they had was real, that the whispers about his wife and children were just that—whispers. And even if they were true, she reasoned, he had chosen her. He wasn't spending his evenings or weekends with Barbara Ann; he was with her, taking her to the finest restaurants, showing her the city, and planning a future she never thought possible back in South Carolina.

Driving through the streets of Baltimore in his Mercedes-Benz, she felt like someone important—someone who had finally escaped the struggles of her past. She'd catch her reflection in the rearview mirror and smile, marveling at how far she'd come.

But the warnings didn't stop. Staff members' sidelong glances became more pointed, and the occasional comment about "Mrs. Carrington" grew harder to ignore. Johnnie Mae, however, was determined not to let anyone ruin what she had. As long as Dr. Carrington was by her side, the rest of the world didn't matter.

PART 3

Chapter 8

An Affair with Ruin

As weeks turned into months, Johnnie Mae settled into her position at Dr. Carrington's practice, though her work ethic began to draw murmurs of disapproval among the staff. Medical billing fell behind, invoices piled up, and crucial supplies were delayed. The staff, already wary of stepping on toes, hesitated to tell Dr. Carrington that his girlfriend wasn't fulfilling her responsibilities.

Johnnie Mae, however, seemed oblivious to the growing discontent. She was distracted—not by the demands of her job, but by the constant stream of phone calls from a particular Medicaid representative. The woman called frequently, asking to speak with Dr. Carrington about billing discrepancies and program updates. Calm and professional yet persistently calling, she made Johnnie Mae uneasy.

One afternoon, after another call from the representative, Johnnie Mae's jealousy got the better of her. "Can I ask you something?" she said abruptly, interrupting the woman.

There was a pause on the other end. "Sure," the representative replied cautiously.

"Do you know Dr. Carrington personally, or is this just... professional?" Johnnie Mae asked, her voice laced with suspicion.

The silence that followed was icy. Then the representative's voice sharpened. "That's none of your business," she said, hanging up.

Johnnie Mae sat at her desk, stunned and fuming. Her insecurity gnawed at her, conjuring scenarios she couldn't control. She had no idea the representative's calls were tied to something much larger than her jealousy.

Unbeknownst to Johnnie Mae, Dr. Carrington had been playing a key role in the rollout of Medicaid programs, particularly those focused on children's oral health. As one of the few prominent Black dentists in Baltimore, he had been instrumental in advocating for better access to care in underserved communities. His influence extended beyond the walls of his practice, shaping policies that would benefit generations to come.

But the mounting administrative chaos—late billing, missing invoices, and backlogged orders—was beginning to catch up with him. Missing payments and delayed reimbursements threatened not only the stability of his practice but also his credibility among colleagues and policymakers. While Johnnie Mae enjoyed the perks of their relationship, her inability to manage the office efficiently was quietly unraveling the foundation of Dr. Carrington's professional empire.

The situation reached a boiling point when Dr. Carrington was summoned to an urgent meeting with Medicaid officials. Questions surfaced about the billing issues, and whispers of mismanagement circulated. For a man whose reputation rested on precision and excellence, these lapses posed a serious threat to everything he'd built.

Yet Dr. Carrington remained blissfully unaware of the storm brewing behind the scenes, preoccupied with juggling his growing responsibilities in Medicaid program rollout and maintaining his dual lives—one with Barbara Ann and another with Johnnie Mae.

But the seeds of trouble had already been sown. The Medicaid representative, whose professional demeanor masked a deeper personal connection to Dr. Carrington, felt humiliated and betrayed by Johnnie Mae's intrusive questioning. Just weeks prior, she had spent a weekend with him at the Village of Cross Keys condo, believing their relationship to be genuine.

For her, Johnnie Mae's insinuation of a romantic rivalry was a slap in the face, a reminder that she was merely another pawn in Dr. Carrington's elaborate web of charm and deception. Anger and hurt quickly eclipsed any lingering affection she felt for him.

Out of both spite and a sense of duty, the Medicaid representative escalated her concerns to her superiors. "I'm worried there may be billing irregularities in Dr. Carrington's practice," she reported. "There have been delays, discrepancies, and unprofessional behavior from his office staff. It might be worth investigating."

Although initially vague, the accusation set off alarm bells. Medicaid audits were no small matter, and for a high-profile dentist like Dr. Carrington—already a central figure in Medicaid policy implementation—any hint of impropriety could have catastrophic consequences.

When the notice of a formal audit arrived at the office, panic set in. A year's worth of minor oversights and Johnnie Mae's growing neglect of her duties had created a perfect storm of errors that now threatened to engulf the practice. Delayed billing, missing documentation, and unfulfilled orders were no longer just internal mishaps; they were potential evidence of fraud.

Blindsided by the audit, Dr. Carrington demanded answers. His staff scrambled to explain, but no one dared point a finger at Johnnie Mae. Meanwhile, she remained oblivious to the chaos, continuing to enjoy shopping trips, luxury dinners, and weekend drives in the Roadster with Dr. Carrington.

As auditors combed through records, Dr. Carrington's carefully curated image of success and integrity began to crack. Whispers of fraud spread quickly, tarnishing his reputation among colleagues and policymakers. While he struggled to contain the fallout, the betrayal—both by Johnnie Mae's negligence and the Medicaid representative's retaliation—was a blow he hadn't anticipated.

As if the pressure weren't enough, that afternoon, Dr. Carrington's son, Russell III, stopped by the dental office and asked Johnnie Mae if he could speak with his dad. Johnnie Mae buzzed the private office. "Your son is here."

"Send him in."

Russell III walked in and sat in the leather chair across from his father's desk, hands clasped as he tried to steady himself. It was the first time he'd come on his own, without his mother scheduling an appointment or orchestrating a chance meeting.

"I turn sixteen next week," Russell III said, getting straight to the point. "I want a car."

Dr. Carrington leaned back, adjusting his cufflinks as he studied the boy—no, the young man—in front of him. He had the same sharp features, the same quiet determination in his eyes that Russell Sr. himself had possessed as a boy.

"A car," Dr. Carrington repeated, tapping his fingers on the desk.

"And what exactly have you done to earn that?"

Russell III shifted in his seat. "I got good grades."

"Good isn't enough," his father countered. "I expect excellence. What's your GPA?"

"3.2."

Dr. Carrington let out a small, unimpressed hum. "Not bad. Not great." He folded his hands. "Do you have a job?"

Russell III hesitated. "Not yet, but I—"

"Then why should I hand you a car?" Dr. Carrington interrupted. "That's a responsibility, not just a gift. You need a job to pay for gas, maintenance, and insurance. What's your plan for the future?"

Russell III exhaled sharply. He'd expected a simple yes or no, not an interrogation.

"I don't know yet," he admitted. "College, maybe."

"Maybe?" Dr. Carrington raised an eyebrow. "That's not an answer, son."

The word son hung between them, unfamiliar and heavy. Russell III clenched his jaw.

"So what? If I don't have straight A's and a five-year plan, I don't deserve anything?" he demanded, frustration creeping into his voice.

Dr. Carrington sighed. "It's not about deserving, Russell. It's about being prepared. I won't set you up for failure. You want a car? Show me you can handle responsibility. Get your grades up. Get a job. Come back to me when you can prove you're ready."

Russell III stood, his chest tight. "Forget it," he muttered. "I shouldn't have come."

Dr. Carrington didn't stop him. He only watched as his son stormed out, wondering if Russell III realized that for the first time, he wasn't shutting him out—he was pushing him forward.

Chapter 9

The Whisper Campaign

The whispers began slowly, spreading like smoke through the tightly knit circles of Baltimore's medical community. At first, they were just murmurs—a hint of trouble at Dr. Carrington's practice, a few questions about delayed reimbursements. But as the Medicaid investigation intensified, the rumors grew louder and more pointed.

"Did you hear? Medicaid's auditing Dr. Carrington's office." "They're saying there might be fraud involved." "Unbelievable. He's such a prominent figure—surely there's been a mistake."

Not everyone was quick to defend him, though. For every supporter, there was someone willing to believe the worst. After all, Dr. Carrington's rise to prominence had not come without making enemies. His polished exterior and unmatched ambition had earned him as many detractors as admirers, and the investigation became fuel for those who had long waited for his downfall.

Inside the office, the tension was palpable. Staff whispered in hushed tones, worried about their livelihoods as the audit uncovered a tangled web of billing discrepancies. Files were missing, payments had been misapplied, and Johnnie Mae's careless record-keeping left glaring gaps that auditors were eager to exploit.

Dr. Carrington, usually calm and collected, began to show signs of strain. He'd always prided himself on maintaining control, but now he felt that control slipping away. Behind closed doors, he confided in a select group of trusted colleagues. "This is just a big mistake," he insisted, pacing the floor of his office. "It's nothing more than record-keeping errors. You know how these bureaucrats are—they're looking for something, anything, to justify their investigation."

His colleagues nodded sympathetically, though some privately wondered if there was more to the story. They'd heard the rumors about his personal life, the lavish spending, and the questionable presence of Johnnie Mae in the office. And while they wanted to believe in his innocence, the mounting evidence was difficult to dismiss.

As the investigation dragged on, Dr. Carrington's paranoia deepened. He became hyper-aware of every glance, every whispered conversation, convinced that people were talking about him. He stopped attending social events and avoided public appearances, fearing the judgment of his peers. Even his lectures—once a source of pride and acclaim—became a burden.

Despite his efforts to project confidence, Dr. Carrington couldn't shake the feeling that the walls were closing in. The investigation wasn't just a threat to his career—it was a threat to the life he'd so carefully built and to the image of success and perfection he'd spent decades cultivating. And the irony wasn't lost on him: the very systems he'd helped shape were now being used to dismantle him.

Chapter 10

The Broken Oath

Dr. Russell Carrington Jr. sat alone in his office late one evening, the shadows stretching across the walls like silent accusations. The once-pristine space, adorned with certificates and accolades, now felt suffocating. The Medicaid fraud investigation had grown more intense, with auditors questioning every file, every payment, every decision. Each inquiry felt like a knife twisting deeper, cutting into the pristine image he had labored so hard to maintain.

Dr. Carrington had built his career on principles of integrity and service, often recalling the oath he took as a dentist: to do no harm, to serve his community, to uphold the highest ethical standards. Yet now, those ideals felt like distant memories, relics of a man he no longer recognized.

The whispers in the medical community had become a roar. Colleagues were distancing themselves. Even Johnnie Mae, oblivious to her role in the chaos, had turned into a source of irritation rather than comfort.

The final straw came when one of his most trusted colleagues confronted him after hours. "Russell," the man said gently, "I've been hearing things. People are saying there's fraud—that your office is submitting false claims to Medicaid. Tell me it's not true."

Dr. Carrington bristled, his paranoia flaring. "It's a misunderstanding," he snapped. "A few errors in record-keeping, that's all. I've got it under control."

Later that night, alone in his office, he stared at the stack of files the auditors had requested. The discrepancies were glaring. Months of neglect, compounded by Johnnie Mae's incompetence, had created a paper trail of errors that would be impossible to explain.

He picked up the phone and dialed a contact he had avoided for the past year—a woman known for her ability to "fix" problems discreetly. "I need some files…reviewed," Dr. Carrington said hesitantly.

The voice on the other end chuckled darkly. "I thought you were never going to call, Sweetie. Guess you're finally finished playing with your little eye candy."

When he hung up, Dr. Carrington felt a wave of nausea. This wasn't who he was—or at least, who he used to be. But the fear of losing everything, of being exposed, outweighed his guilt. He tried to rationalize the decision, telling himself it was the only way to set things right.

Desperate, he realized there was only one person who could truly salvage the situation: Elsie Johnson.

Elsie had once been the backbone of his office before he fired her to make room for Johnnie Mae. She was professional, meticulous, and, most importantly, loyal—until their personal relationship complicated matters. Calling her now was a bitter pill to swallow, but he had no choice.

"I'll come back—for the office, not for you," Elsie said flatly over the phone. "But let's be clear: I'm in charge of getting this place in order, and you'll stay out of my way."

Dr. Carrington agreed, swallowing his pride. The next morning, Elsie walked into the office with her head held high, her mere presence commanding respect. She wasted no time assessing the damage, organizing files, and delegating tasks. The staff, relieved to see someone competent at the helm, quickly fell in line.

Johnnie Mae, however, was livid. From the moment Elsie arrived, Johnnie Mae felt her position slipping away—both professionally and personally. She noticed the unspoken history between Dr. Carrington and Elsie in the way they avoided each other's gaze, in how he deferred to Elsie's authority.

The final blow came when Johnnie Mae overheard Elsie telling Dr. Carrington, "This wouldn't have happened if you hadn't let her run the office into the ground. You let your personal life ruin everything."

Humiliated and furious, Johnnie Mae confronted Dr. Carrington that evening.

"So this is how it ends?" she demanded. "You call in your ex to clean up your mess, and I'm just supposed to sit here and watch?"

Dr. Carrington, exhausted and cornered, tried to placate her. "This isn't about us, Johnnie Mae. It's about saving the practice. You knew you were struggling with the office work—"

"Don't you dare put this on me!" she snapped, tears brimming in her eyes. "You brought me into this, and now you're blaming me for everything?"

She didn't wait for an answer. Grabbing her things, she turned to him one last time. "Enjoy your perfect little office with your perfect little ex-girlfriend. We're done."

Johnnie Mae stormed out, slamming the door behind her. For the first time, Russell didn't chase her. Instead, he sat alone in his office, the weight of his decisions pressing down on him.

Though Johnnie Mae continued to show up for work, Elsie was fully in control. Under her leadership, the office began to stabilize—but the damage to Dr. Carrington's personal life was irreparable. The woman who once idolized him now despised him, and the looming scandal over his practice continued to grow.

Chapter 11

Fragile Victory

The day the Medicaid auditors closed their investigation, the office was unusually quiet. After weeks of scrutiny and tense meetings, the lead investigator finally delivered the verdict: the issues stemmed from poor record-keeping, not deliberate fraud. Thanks to Elsie Johnson's tireless effort to organize the chaos, the auditors left satisfied that all errors had been addressed.

Dr. Carrington managed to avoid a public scandal and was allowed to plead guilty to minor administrative oversights without significant punishment. He would pay a fine and undergo a brief compliance review, but his license and reputation remained intact—for now.

As the staff celebrated the good news, Russell sat alone in his office, staring at his reflection in a framed certificate. The man looking back didn't feel like the celebrated dentist or community leader; he felt like a fraud—not because of the investigation, but because he had compromised everything he once believed in.

Despite the reprieve, Dr. Carrington couldn't let go of what had led to the investigation. His thoughts kept returning to Johnnie Mae, replaying every mistake she had made and every careless oversight. To him, she was the reason his empire had nearly crumbled.

"She was supposed to help me," he said, pacing his office. "I gave her everything—money, a job, a place in my life—and this is how she repays me? By almost ruining everything I've worked for?" His bitterness toward Johnnie Mae grew with each passing day. He confided in a few close colleagues, painting her as an ungrateful and incompetent distraction. "She almost destroyed my career," he told them. "I should've known better than to mix business with…personal matters."

The whispers began to circulate, tarnishing Johnnie Mae's reputation. Though she had already left his life, his influence still lingered, making it difficult for her to move on.

Meanwhile, Elsie Johnson remained at the office, restoring it to its former efficiency. Though she kept their interactions strictly professional, Russell couldn't ignore the disdain in her eyes whenever she spoke to him. He knew she had returned to fix the mess, not for him, and that knowledge stung more than he cared to admit.

On the surface, life at the practice returned to normal. The office ran smoothly, the investigation was over, and Dr. Carrington's career continued. But beneath the surface, cracks were forming. His colleagues noticed his growing paranoia, and his staff tiptoed around his volatile moods.

For Dr. Carrington, the real punishment wasn't in the courtroom or from the investigation; it was in the slow erosion of his sense of self. He realized that the man he had become was a far cry from the man he once aspired to be.

By the end of 1971, the chaos of the Medicaid investigation had faded into memory, though its scars remained. Dr. Carrington's dental practice, once on the brink of ruin, began to recover. The addition of Dr. Harding—a bright, eager graduate of Meharry Medical School—brought much-needed relief. Harding's enthusiasm and fresh perspective reinvigorated the office, and his ability to manage a large portion of the patient load allowed Dr. Carrington to take a step back. Orthodontist Gwendolyn Dunn, who had taken a brief hiatus during the turbulent months of the investigation, returned to full capacity, adding further stability. Working together, they navigated the demanding schedule, treating the 40 to 60 patients who passed through the doors each day. Patients who had doubted the practice during the investigation gradually returned, reassured by the staff's professionalism.

Despite the newfound normalcy, Dr. Carrington was preoccupied with personal matters. On Christmas Eve, his 17-year-old son, Russell Carrington III, paid him a visit and announced that he was about to become a father.

"The baby is due in mid-January," Russell III said nervously, glancing at his father. "We're planning for the delivery that weekend."

Dr. Carrington stared at his son for a long moment before nodding. "You'll handle this responsibly," he said in a measured tone. "It's time for you to step up."

Though he appeared calm, the news left Dr. Carrington unsettled. At 38, he was about to become a grandfather, a stark reminder of how quickly time was passing.

Meanwhile, Johnnie Mae's time in Baltimore was drawing to a close. After leaving the apartment Dr. Carrington had purchased for her, she moved in with her sister, quietly planning her return to Chester, South Carolina. Her relationship with Dr. Carrington was long over, and the glamour that once surrounded them had dissolved. She missed her daughter and longed for the simplicity of life in the South, far from the whispers and judgment she endured in Baltimore.

Although she didn't speak to him directly, she left a note at the office addressed to Dr. Carrington:

Thank you for everything you did for me. I'm going back home to be with my family. I hope you find what you're looking for. Take care.

Dr. Carrington read the note in his office, his face unreadable. He folded it carefully and placed it in his desk drawer, uncertain why he chose to keep it.

As 1971 came to a close, Russell reflected on the year's events. The Medicaid investigation had served as a wake-up call, forcing him to confront the fragility of his reputation and the ramifications of his decisions. Yet, as always, he managed to land on his feet, maintaining his perfect smile, his image of success, and the veneer of stability.

He thought about how his grandson's birth in January of 1972 would mark the start of a new chapter in his life—a reminder of the passage of time. He vowed to focus on his family and his practice, reassuring himself that the worst was behind him.

But deep down, he couldn't shake the feeling that his newfound peace was only temporary—a fragile calm before the next storm.

The New Year arrived with a sense of optimism that Dr. Carrington welcomed. The practice was running smoothly, and the turmoil of the past year felt like a distant memory. While preparing for a dinner party at his Cross Keys condo, Dr. Carrington allowed himself a rare moment of satisfaction.

That morning, he received a phone call from his son.

"Dad, the baby's here!" Russell III said excitedly. "Priscilla gave birth to a healthy baby boy—seven pounds, three ounces. We named him

Russell H. Carrington IV."

Dr. Carrington leaned back in his chair, a wide smile spreading across his face. "That's wonderful news, son. Congratulations to both of you," he said, pausing to savor the moment. "Bring the baby boy to the office on Monday—I want to meet my grandson."

For the first time in months, Dr. Carrington felt renewed hope for the future. The thought of holding the next generation of his family filled him with pride.

By the time the dinner party began that evening, Dr. Carrington was in high spirits. His Cross Keys condo looked immaculate, the table set with fine china and crystal. The guests included colleagues and friends who both admired and respected him.

Throughout the evening, he moved effortlessly around the room, greeting guests and ensuring everyone felt welcome. His date for the night—a poised, elegant woman from the dental board—remained close by, enhancing his image of success and charm.

All that changed when Johnnie Mae walked in.

She appeared radiant, her smile confident as she approached Dr. Carrington with a tall, sharply dressed man on her arm.

"Dr. Carrington," she said, her voice warm but firm, "I'd like you to meet Michael. Michael, this is Dr. Carrington."

Dr. Carrington's gaze flicked between them, his mind racing. Seeing Johnnie Mae with another man hit him like a gut punch, but he quickly masked his reaction, extending his hand.

"Pleasure to meet you," he said, his tone steady but clipped.

Michael shook his hand firmly and offered a polite smile. "I've heard a lot about you, Dr. Carrington."

"Have you?" Russell replied, a subtle edge to his voice.

Johnnie Mae noticed the tension but remained composed, introducing Michael to the other guests before moving on.

For the rest of the evening, Russell's attention veered between his social obligations and the sight of Johnnie Mae laughing with Michael. The ease with which she had seemingly moved on stung more deeply than he cared to admit.

His companion noticed his irritation and leaned in. "Everything alright?"

Dr. Carrington forced a smile. "Of course. Just a lot on my mind."

But as the evening progressed, his mood darkened. Every shared laugh between Johnnie Mae and Michael felt like a provocation, and every glance she threw in Russell's direction was a reminder of what he had lost—and would never regain.

Though the party ended without incident, Dr. Carrington's thoughts remained elsewhere as the last guest departed. Alone with his overnight guest in his condo, he poured them both a drink and stared out at the city lights.

He was certain Johnnie Mae's appearance had been calculated—she wanted him to see that she had moved on, that she no longer needed him. Yet the sight of her with someone else unsettled him in ways he couldn't fully articulate.

Earlier that day, the birth of his grandson had filled him with joy, but now that happiness felt overshadowed by the night's events. Once again, his personal and professional lives were colliding, pulling him in opposite directions.

As he finished his drink, Russell made a silent vow: he would never allow anyone—not Johnnie Mae or anyone else—to undermine his image or legacy again.

But deep down, he couldn't ignore the nagging fear that the cracks in his façade were already starting to show—

Ms. Johnnie Mae Warren & Date

Chapter 12

Behind Closed Doors

The following Monday, the hum of normalcy returned as Dr. Carrington and his staff reconvened at the office. Patients lined the waiting area, staff shuffled through files, and the phones rang incessantly—a typical start to the week. Yet, for Dr. Carrington, nothing about this Monday felt routine.

His emotions from Saturday night lingered, casting a shadow over his mood. The combination of becoming a grandfather and Johnnie Mae's unexpected appearance with Michael left him grappling with conflicting feelings of pride, loss, and simmering resentment.

Late in the morning, Russell III arrived at the office with baby Russell H. Carrington IV cradled in his arms. Staff members gathered around, cooing at the infant, while Dr. Carrington stood back, watching with a mix of pride and detachment.

When his son handed him the baby, Dr. Carrington hesitated for a moment before taking the child into his arms. The baby looked up at him, his tiny features resembling those of his son at that age.

"Well," Russell said with a faint smile, "he's a fine-looking boy."

The room filled with warm chatter as the staff congratulated Russell III and took turns admiring the baby. For a moment, the tension that had been plaguing Dr. Carrington seemed to lift, replaced by a rare feeling of familial connection.

As Russell III prepared to leave, Dr. Carrington placed a hand on his shoulder. "Take care of your family," he said firmly. "This is your responsibility now."

"Yes, sir," his son replied, sensing the weight of his father's expectations.

Despite the brief reprieve, the events of Saturday night still gnawed at Dr. Carrington. He couldn't shake the image of Johnnie Mae and Michael, their easy smiles and obvious chemistry. It felt like a deliberate affront, a reminder that she had moved on while he remained tethered to his carefully constructed but increasingly fragile world.

As the day wore on, his irritation began to seep into his interactions with the staff. He snapped at the other receptionist, Elsie, for a minor scheduling error and dismissed Dr. Harding's suggestion for a new procedure without consideration.

By the afternoon, Gwendolyn Dunn, the orthodontist, approached him in his office.

"Russell," she began, closing the door behind her, "is everything all right?"

He looked up from his desk, his expression guarded. "Why wouldn't it be?"

"Because you've been on edge all day," she replied. "We've all noticed it. If there's something going on, you can talk to us."

Dr. Carrington sighed and leaned back in his chair. "It's nothing, Gwendolyn. Just a lot on my mind. Let's focus on the patients."

She nodded but didn't press further. As she left, Dr. Carrington stared out the window, his thoughts returning to Johnnie Mae.

That evening, as the office quieted and the last patient left, Dr. Carrington called for Elsie Johnson and Johnnie Mae to come to his office.

His mind was preoccupied as the two women stepped in. "Have a seat!" he said. The atmosphere turned ominous when they realized Dr. Carrington was holding a .38 revolver in one hand and locking the door with the other. With a single question, he demanded, "Why did you come?"

He knew Johnnie Mae's appearance at the dinner party wasn't a coincidence. Whether it was intentional or not, her presence had unsettled him, forcing him to confront emotions he thought he'd buried.

The lingering bitterness and jealousy gnawed at him, even as he told himself he had no right to feel this way. He had ended things with her, and yet, the thought of her moving on felt like a betrayal.

The tension was palpable in Dr. Carrington's office as Elsie and Johnnie Mae stood before him, trapped in the suffocating space. Both women had their eyes wide with a mix of confusion and apprehension, unsure of what had just transpired.

"I gave her everything!" Dr. Carrington yelled again, his voice trembling with rage. His hands shook as he gripped the revolver. "Everything! And this is how she repays me—by leaving, by... humiliating me. After all I've done, after all I've given her, she turns her back on me. She ruins my life."

Elsie glanced nervously at Johnnie Mae, whose expression was unreadable. Still, she could see the tension in Johnnie Mae's shoulders, the anxiety in the way she stood.

"Russell, calm down," Elsie urged, though her own voice quivered.

She had never seen him like this before. "This isn't the way to handle things. You can't—"

He ignored her, his eyes locked on Johnnie Mae. "You listen to me," Dr. Carrington snapped. "You only have two choices—stay here with me, or die."

His words hung in the air like a poisonous fog. Elsie's heart skipped a beat. She had seen him angry before, but never this cold, never this dangerous.

Johnnie Mae, for the first time, stood her ground, her lips pressed into a tight line. She felt the weight of his gaze but refused to let him see her falter.

"Don't think you can control me," Johnnie Mae said, her voice steady despite the flicker of fear in her eyes. "I'm done with you, Russell. You can't make me stay, and you sure as hell can't threaten me into submission."

Russell's face twisted in disbelief. He stepped closer, his voice rising. "You think you can just walk away from me? You think I'll let you ruin everything I've worked for? After everything I've given you—this is how you repay me?"

The room felt smaller, the walls closing in. Elsie took a step back, not knowing what to do or how to stop the escalating madness. She had always been the one to clean up Russell's messes, but this was beyond anything she had ever witnessed.

Dr. Carrington's eyes flickered toward Elsie. His anger, though still boiling, shifted into something darker. "Tell her, Elsie. Tell her she doesn't have a choice."

Elsie's mouth went dry. Her mind raced, but the fear gnawing at her made it hard to think. She had never been afraid of Russell before, but this evening felt different. She knew he was capable of dangerous things, and she had seen the cracks in his façade. But to witness him like this—unhinged and desperate—was unsettling.

"I—I can't, Russell," Elsie stammered, shaking her head. "You're not thinking clearly."

Dr. Carrington's face turned red with fury, his jaw clenching as he turned away. He walked to the sofa in his office. "Then I'll make her understand. She's mine, and I'll make her stay. No one walks away from me. No one."

Elsie watched helplessly, her instincts screaming at her to intervene before this escalated any further. But she knew the power Dr. Carrington held, the grip he maintained over everyone in his orbit. And in this moment, she feared for all of them.

Johnnie Mae's heart pounded in her chest as she took a step forward. "You don't get to control me anymore," she said, her voice a little firmer now, even though the threat in the room was palpable. "I've had enough of your games, Dr. Carrington. I'm done. And if you think you can scare me into staying, you're mistaken."

For a moment, Dr. Carrington just stared at her, as if trying to process her defiance. But the words from earlier—the threat of life and death—still lingered in the room, dark and unforgiving.

"I can make you stay," he muttered under his breath, more to himself than to her.

Elise, desperate to defuse the situation, stepped in. "Russell, please, this has gone too far. Let's just—"

"No," he snapped. "She needs to understand. She's been nothing but trouble for me, and she's going to learn what happens when you mess with me."

As the confrontation built, something shifted in the room—a tension too thick to ignore. Johnnie Mae stood firm, her gaze unwavering. She knew she was no longer in control of the situation, but she wasn't about to let Russell tear her down again.

"I'm not afraid of you," she said quietly, her words underlined by conviction. "And I'm not going to stay. I've learned enough about you to know exactly what kind of man you are. I don't need you."

Dr. Carrington's chest rose and fell with heavy breaths. Frustration, betrayal, and anger swirled within him in a dangerous mix. His mind raced, and in a moment of panic, he reached for his phone, dialing a number without thinking.

But before he could speak, Elise placed a hand on his arm. "Russell, this isn't the way. You're going to destroy everything—your reputation, your practice... and worse, you'll destroy yourself. Don't make this worse than it already is."

Dr. Carrington pulled away, frustration boiling over into something darker. He wasn't used to feeling so out of control. He wasn't used to being challenged.

His hands trembled as he dialed his father's number. Russell Sr. had always been a figure of authority in his life—the one man he both feared and revered. Maybe, just maybe, his father could make sense of this chaos.

"Russell," his father answered on the third ring, voice steady and calm. "What's going on?"

"I need you here," Dr. Carrington said, his voice raw, edged with desperation. "I'm holding Johnnie Mae in my office... I... I need help. You have to come."

There was a long pause on the other end. "What are you talking about, son?" Russell Sr.'s voice deepened, confusion and concern creeping through. "What's going on?"

"I've made mistakes, Dad," Dr. Carrington whispered, his breath catching. "She's trying to ruin everything I've worked for. She's leaving me. I can't let her go. You have to get here—now."

Silence stretched before Russell Sr. spoke again, more firmly this time. "Hold tight, son. I'm on my way. Don't do anything rash."

As tension inside Dr. Carrington's office thickened, word began to spread among the staff. Whispers turned into phone calls, and soon rumors buzzed through the streets outside Garwyn Medical Center. Onlookers gathered on the sidewalk, drawn by the sudden drama surrounding the once-respected dentist and community figure.

Within minutes, police cars pulled up to the curb, sirens subdued but urgent. Officers filed out, and the strain in the air grew heavier as they approached the building.

Inside, Dr. Carrington paced, his mind spiraling. Each past decision felt like a chain tightening around him.

A soft knock on the door. "Dr. Carrington?" called a calm, authoritative voice from the other side. "This is Officer Louis Witte. We need to talk."

He didn't respond right away; his father wasn't there yet. The room felt like it was closing in on him, and his emotions whirled in a storm of rage, fear, and uncertainty.

The knock came again, louder. "We're not here to hurt you," Officer Witte said, his tone steady but firm. "We just want to make sure you and everyone inside are okay. Let us help you."

Dr. Carrington's grip tightened on the pistol at the sound of the officer's voice, the weight of his choices bearing down on him.

"Let me talk to the ladies," Officer Witte called out, sensing the tension. "Let us mediate. There's no reason for anyone to get hurt here."

Elise stood in the corner, exchanging a look with Johnnie Mae. Fear was etched into their faces. This had escalated far beyond a lover's quarrel or a business dispute.

Just then, Dr. Carrington's office phone rang. It was his father, just as promised.

"Russell, I'm outside," came his father's clipped, urgent voice. "Now open the door."

Dr. Carrington wiped sweat from his brow and walked to unlock the door. His father stepped into the hallway, cutting through the tension with his presence. Russell Sr.'s eyes flicked to his son.

"Dad, I—I didn't know what else to do," Dr. Carrington stammered, voice trembling as he backed away from the door. "She was leaving me... she tried to ruin everything."

Russell Sr. didn't respond right away. He stepped into the office, assessing Johnnie Mae and Elise with practiced calm before turning back to his son.

"You've lost control, Russell," he said quietly, disappointment in his voice. "And you've dragged all of us into this mess."

Dr. Carrington's eyes filled with anger and frustration, but he swallowed it. "I didn't mean for it to get this far, but she just—she ruined me."

Russell Sr. shook his head. "You've ruined yourself, son. You let your ego, your anger, get the best of you. And now look at the disaster you've created."

Police radios crackled outside, the sense of urgency intensifying. Dr. Carrington felt cornered on all sides, paranoia eating at him.

"Russell," his father said, voice low but firm. "You need to end this now. Open the door, let them in. Let's get you out of this. If you don't, you're going to lose everything."

The weight of his father's words struck harder than any accusation. Dr. Carrington's hands shook as he looked at Johnnie Mae and Elise.

Finally, without a word, he stepped back and unlocked the office door, disarming himself as officers entered. Two of Dr. Carrington's colleagues came in, hoping to talk him into surrendering. Officer Witte volunteered himself as a hostage, continually urging Dr. Carrington to surrender. Another colleague, Dr. Shirley Clinton, appeared and asked to speak with Dr. Carrington. He agreed, on the condition that Officer Witte leave the room.

Officer Witte asked for the gun. Dr. Carrington replied, "In a couple of minutes."

The tension in the office was unbearable, the air thick with fear and anger as Dr. Carrington's world dangled on the brink. Dr. Clinton, a trusted colleague who had seen the fractures in Dr. Carrington's once-impeccable façade, tried to mediate. As he sat across from Dr. Carrington, speaking in a soft, measured voice, Dr. Carrington remained eerily silent, his mind teeming with dark thoughts.

"Russell," Dr. Clinton said gently, concern evident in every word, "you don't have to do this. Let them go. They'll listen, but you need to calm down before it's too late."

But it was already too late. In those few moments of conversation, the weight of his past choices destroyed the last of Dr. Carrington's composure. He wasn't just angry; he was consumed by something darker.

Outside, Dr. Donald Stewart stood near the ranking officer, arms crossed as he pleaded for a chance to talk sense into Dr. Carrington. "Look, I know him better than anyone," Dr. Stewart insisted. "Let me go in there—maybe I can end this before somebody gets hurt."

The officer hesitated, then nodded. "You've got five minutes, Doc."

Dr. Stewart exhaled sharply and walked through the glass doors. His footsteps echoed down the hallway as he approached Dr. Carrington's office. He knocked once before pushing the door open.

Inside, Dr. Carrington stood behind his desk, his normally pristine suit disheveled, his tie loosened. He clutched a pistol—something Dr. Stewart had never known him to carry. The hostages sat frozen in fear.

"Russ," Dr. Stewart began carefully, hands raised in a calming gesture. "It's me."

Dr. Carrington's gaze was distant. Rage and desperation clouded his once-sharp eyes.

"I can't let them take everything from me, Donald," he muttered, shaking his head. "Not after everything I've built."

Dr. Stewart inched forward. "Nobody's taking anything, man. But this? This isn't the way."

Dr. Carrington let out a bitter laugh. "What choice do I have? They want to ruin me. They want to tear down everything I worked for—my practice, my reputation. You know what they all say about me. They always wanted to see me fall."

Dr. Stewart felt his stomach twist. He had seen Russell angry, but never like this. "You're not thinking straight, Russ. You're one of the best doctors in this city. You don't have to go out like this."

Dr. Carrington's jaw clenched, his breathing unsteady. "It's too late."

Dr. Stewart swallowed. He'd known Dr. Carrington all his life, but the man before him was a stranger. He realized he couldn't get through.

With a slow, resigned nod, Dr. Stewart backed away. "I tried."

He left the office, the heavy door clicking shut behind him. Outside, the chilly Baltimore air hit him like a slap. Police and onlookers stared expectantly.

Dr. Stewart exhaled. "He's lost his damn mind," he murmured.

Suddenly, the office door burst open. Elise Johnson raced out, her face pale and frantic, followed by Johnnie Mae, her body taut with fear and determination. They didn't stop; they had one goal—escape.

Dr. Carrington, sensing his last shreds of control slipping away, chased them down the hallway. Adrenaline surged through his veins as he clutched the gun, anger and betrayal burning inside him. His career, reputation, and the women who had defied him—all seemed to be falling away at once.

"Don't you dare leave me!" he shouted, voice shaking with desperation. Eyes wild, he raised the gun and fired two shots in quick succession.

The first shot struck Johnnie Mae in the back, sending her reeling. She cried out and collapsed in another reception room, her legs folding beneath her. The second shot hit her again, and she fell against the wall, gasping, "Please don't kill me."

Elise's scream ripped through the corridor, drowned in the chaos unfolding around them. Dr. Carrington, his mind clouded by rage, advanced with lethal intent.

Then a single shot rang out from behind him, echoing through the hallway. Dr. Carrington felt a piercing pain in his chest as the bullet struck. His hand went slack, the gun clattering to the floor. Staggering back, his vision blurred, he looked up to see Officer Witte standing in the doorway, firearm still raised.

"Drop the weapon, Dr. Carrington," the officer commanded, urgency in his voice. "It's over."

Dr. Carrington stumbled, blood soaking his shirt. His knees gave out, and he collapsed. In one last act of desperation, he fired another shot, missing Officer Witte but critically wounding a private security guard.

Elise rushed to Johnnie Mae, hands shaking as she tried in vain to stop the bleeding. Johnnie Mae's breaths came in shallow gasps. She looked at Elise with confusion and pain in her eyes. "I... I didn't want this," she whispered, her voice fading as she was pronounced dead minutes later.

Officer Witte stepped forward, his expression somber. "It's too late, Dr. Carrington," he said quietly. "You can't run from what you've done."

Sirens screamed outside, the red and blue lights dancing against the walls of Garwyn Medical Center. Dr. Carrington's world had collapsed, and in those final moments, the weight of his choices crushed him. He had taken lives, destroyed his legacy, and now it all slipped away.

BEHIND THIS DOOR – ROOM 211 for 2hours, Dr. Russell H. Carrington Jr. held Jonnie Mae Warren and his nurse at gunpoint

Chapter 13

Fractured Legacy

The media frenzy that followed was swift and unforgiving. News outlets swarmed the streets outside Garwyn Medical Center, reporting on the shocking turn of events. Dr. Carrington, once a respected figure in the community, now became the subject of a nationwide scandal. His career, his reputation, his legacy—all shattered in an instant.

Elise, too, was emotionally and physically shaken, having witnessed the brutal events unfold before her eyes.

The once-proud dentist—whose ambitions had led him to the peak of success—became a tragic symbol of what happens when power, pride, and obsession collide.

The aftermath of that night rippled through Baltimore and beyond. The impact of Dr. Carrington's actions would be felt by his family, his colleagues, and the community for years to come. His fall from grace would remain a cautionary tale of how quickly a life can spiral into darkness.

It had taken him years to build his empire—years of sacrifice, ambition, and carefully constructed alliances. Now, he had to make a choice that would define his legacy. He had already made the decision, but seeing it in writing made it permanent.

He signed his name, sealing the fate of those who would inherit his wealth and those who would not.

The Inheritance

Dr. Carrington left the bulk of his estate—including his lucrative dental practice, real estate holdings, and investment portfolio—to his three children with Barbara Ann. To them, he bequeathed his legacy: the tangible proof of his life's work. He wanted them to carry on with stability, to benefit from the advantages he had fought for, the wealth he had accumulated, and the reputation he had built.

But for Russell III, his eldest son, and for Barbara Ann—the woman who had once shared his bed and his dreams—there was nothing.

The Exclusion

To the outside world, it might have seemed cruel. But to Dr. Carrington, it was a calculated and necessary act.

Russell III had rejected the values Dr. Carrington had tried to instill in him, choosing a path that, in his father's eyes, lacked discipline and ambition. There had been conflicts, bitter words over the years. Dr. Carrington saw no reason to reward what he viewed as rebellion and defiance.

As for Barbara Ann, the exclusion was even more deliberate. She had been there at the beginning, when he was just a man with a dream and a sharp set of dental tools. She had stood by him, loved him, borne his children. But love had not been enough. Over time, they became estranged shadows of what they once were.

At the end of the will, he added a handwritten note—one final message to those left behind:

"To those I have provided for, may you use what I leave wisely. To those I have left out, understand that life is built on choices. These are mine."

His legacy was set.

Chapter 14

Reflection in the Mirror

The sterile, cold air of the hospital seemed to echo with a heaviness that Dr. Carrington's death had left behind. Russell Sr. stood in the corridor, his hands folded tightly in front of him as he stared down at the floor. It had been years since he had seen his son like this—on the edge of ruin—and even though Dr. Carrington's fall was tragic, there was something deeply unsettling about standing here now, in the aftermath of it all.

The nurses and doctors had long moved on to their next duties, leaving Russell Sr. alone with his son's body. The faint hum of machines in the background felt distant, a stark contrast to the silence that hung in the air. He had known that this moment would come— perhaps not in this exact way—but somewhere deep inside, he had been preparing for it for years. His son's reckless path had led him to this point.

As Russell Sr. made arrangements to claim his son's body, the phone rang, its shrill tone breaking the hush of the hospital room. He answered it with a curt "Hello?"

"Is this Russell Carrington Sr.?" The voice on the other end was sharp, with an air of authority.

"Yes," Russell Sr. replied, still somewhat distracted by the sterile environment around him.

"I'm Detective Harris from the Baltimore Police Department," the voice continued. "We received a call from a woman named Barbara Ann. She's claiming to be Dr. Carrington's wife and says she hasn't been notified of his death. Is that true?"

The words hit Russell Sr. like a sudden wave. "Barbara Ann?" he repeated, disbelief creeping into his voice. "I didn't even know if they were still married. They were on and off for years." He paused, glancing down at his son's body. "I had no idea."

Detective Harris's voice stayed calm, but confusion lingered. "She's very upset about not being informed. She says she has a right to know and that no one reached out to her. I just wanted to clarify—do you have any information about this?"

Russell Sr. hesitated, the phone still clutched in his hand. "Look, I don't know what's going on here. My son has always been private about their marriage and their children, and I... I never asked about it."

Detective Harris let out a soft sigh. "Understood. But it seems we need to resolve this situation. Mrs. Carrington is asking to see the body and make arrangements for burial, but we need to confirm her relationship to the deceased before proceeding."

Standing in the hospital corridor, the weight of the moment felt heavier than ever. His son's life had been cut short in a violent, tragic way, and now a new chapter of confusion and chaos was unfolding. It wasn't just about the fallout from Dr. Carrington's actions anymore—it was about who had the right to make decisions on his behalf, who truly had the claim over his estate, his body, and his legacy.

He didn't want to deal with any of it right now. His son's death had already taken too much from him. But the detective's words lingered. Barbara Ann... His son had never been forthcoming about the details of that marriage, but Russell Sr. had always suspected there were unresolved feelings between them. They had fought bitterly over the years, but had they ever truly separated? Or had they just been putting on a façade for everyone, including him?

A knot tightened in his stomach. He didn't want to be dragged into his son's tangled relationships, but now he had no choice.

He stood in the hallway a moment longer, then decided to call his son's home. Though he had already notified Russell III of his father's passing, he needed more information. He needed to hear from his grandson—someone who had been close to Dr. Carrington—what the truth might be.

When Russell III answered, his voice was hoarse, as though he'd been crying. "Granddad, what's going on? They told me Dad is… gone."

Closing his eyes, feeling the loss like a physical weight, Russell Sr. said, "Yes, son. He's gone. I'm here at the hospital, but there's something you need to know. Detective Harris from the police department called me. Barbara Ann says she's still your father's wife, and she's demanding to be informed about everything. I didn't know what to tell her."

Silence stretched on the other end until Russell III spoke, frustration creeping into his tone. "Granddad, I… I don't know what to say. My dad never talked to me about Mrs. Barbara Ann. He kept it private. But I guess I should've known something was off. I never knew for sure whether they were together, but he kept me at a distance from her and the other kids. He didn't mention her after he… after he started seeing other people."

Russell Sr. sighed, the weight of the situation pressing down even harder. "What do you think we should do?"

"I don't know, Grandpa," Russell III replied softly. "But if she says she's his wife, I guess we need to let her handle the funeral. Just… just make sure we're included. Dad might've made his mistakes, but we're his family."

Russell Sr. nodded. "I'll handle it. I'll make sure everything is taken care of."

As the call ended, he stared down at his son's body once more. The path to closure now felt even more complicated than he had anticipated. It wasn't just a matter of Dr. Carrington's death; it was a matter of conflicting claims, unanswered questions, and the tangled web of relationships that had come to light.

In the days to come, the legal battles would unfold, and the questions surrounding Dr. Carrington's legacy—who had the right to control his estate, his assets, and his final wishes—would continue to create a storm of uncertainty. Barbara Ann, despite her estrangement from Dr. Carrington, would fight for her place in his story.

But that was a battle for another day. For now, Russell Sr. would make the arrangements, standing firm in the face of his son's demise and, perhaps for the first time, confronting the deep, unspoken truths that had always lingered beneath the surface of the Carrington family.

A Final Farewell

On the brisk morning of Saturday, January 22, 1972, the towering stone façade of Metropolitan Methodist Church stood solemnly against the gray sky, a silent witness to a community gathering to bid farewell to one of its most complicated figures. Dr. Russell Carrington Jr. had been a man of brilliance, ambition, and undeniable charm—but his life had also been shadowed by scandal, tragedy, and the choices that led to his untimely demise.

The church at the corner of Lanvale and Carrollton Avenue was filled to capacity with hundreds of attendees, including political leaders, medical professionals, and members of Baltimore's Black elite. The atmosphere was heavy, the murmurs of whispered conversations blending with the low strains of the organ as mourners took their seats.

Dr. Carrington, dressed in a gray double-breasted pinstriped suit and matching tie, was laid in state in a conservative gray metal coffin.

The Reverend Ernest P. Clark, a respected figure in the city, stood at the pulpit with the quiet authority of a man who had seen it all—births, weddings, and far too many funerals. He began with a prayer, his voice resonant and measured, carrying through the grand sanctuary.

"We gather here today not to pass judgment, but to remember the life of Dr. Russell Carrington Jr.," Reverend Clark began. "A man who dedicated himself to the care of others, who broke barriers in a segregated world, and who, like all of us, struggled with the complexities of being human."

His words were chosen carefully, striking a balance between acknowledging Dr. Carrington's accomplishments and alluding to the challenges that had marked his final years. He spoke of Dr. Carrington's contributions to oral health, his role in shaping Medicaid policies, and his efforts to uplift the Black community through his work.

But as Reverend Clark's voice filled the church, there was no denying the tension that hung in the air. Among the mourners sat those who had been closest to Dr. Carrington—and those who had been hurt by him.

Barbara Ann sat in the front pew, her face composed but her eyes betraying the storm of emotions she held inside. Despite their estrangement, she had chosen to be here, determined to ensure that her husband's legacy—flawed as it was—would be honored.

Behind her sat Russell Carrington III, his young son, Russell IV, cradled in his arms. The baby was only a week old, oblivious to the gravity of the moment. Russell III's face was set in a mixture of grief and quiet determination, bearing the weight of his father's legacy.

Further back in the church, whispers passed among colleagues and acquaintances. Some spoke of Dr. Carrington's brilliance; others of the scandals that had plagued him. A few exchanged furtive glances when Johnnie Mae's name was mentioned.

Reverend Clark's voice rose, passionate and clear, as he reached the core of his message:

"As you think of our friend who has gone away, you can say he was no worse than the worst of us, and no better than the best of us. Please remember we are not gods to judge this man. He sought out what we all seek—self-power.

"He sought prestige. He sought possession. But what man in this congregation doesn't? He provided a beautiful home on Arrowhead Road for his children.

"There are many things he was not, but now I want to talk about the things he was. Russell left a legacy to you in the form of a lesson. His life, his mistakes, his achievements, and his downfall can be found in the book of life—the Bible."

Reverend Clark turned to Dr. Carrington's colleagues. "Brothers of the professional life, you can't win it all. It all wasn't meant for you to have. He did what he did because he was afraid of not trying enough, and it turned on him. You need God."

The Procession

PROCESSION of professional persons who were among the mourner's attending the Saturday services for Dr. Russell H. Carrington Jr. included dentist, physicians, pharmacist, co-workers and associates.

Following the service, the mourners filed out of the church in a solemn procession. The pallbearers, including some of Dr. Carrington's closest colleagues, carried the casket to the waiting hearse. Outside, a cold wind swept through the crowd, but they remained, their eyes fixed on the hearse as it began its journey to the cemetery.

Among the mourners, conversations continued in hushed tones. Some reflected on Dr. Carrington's legacy, others on the scandals that had overshadowed it. For many, this day marked the end of an era—a final chapter in the life of a man who had been both a shining star and a cautionary tale.

A Quiet Reflection

As the crowd dispersed, Russell Sr. lingered outside the church, his hands tucked into the pockets of his coat. He stared at the departing hearse, lost in thought. He had seen his son rise to incredible heights and fall just as spectacularly. And now, he was gone, leaving behind a legacy as complicated as the man himself.

Russell III approached him, his expression unreadable. "I'm going to make sure my dad's story is told," he said quietly. "The good and the bad. People need to know who he was—all of him."

Russell Sr. nodded but said nothing. He wasn't sure how he felt about the idea of his son's life being laid bare for the world to see. But deep down, he knew it was inevitable. Dr. Carrington's story wasn't just his own—it was a reflection of a community, a time, and a struggle for greatness in the face of immense challenges.

As the church doors closed behind them, the streets of Baltimore seemed quieter than usual. The city had lost one of its brightest—and most troubled—sons. For those who had known him, one question lingered: How would history remember Dr. Russell Carrington Jr.? As a visionary, a flawed man, or something in between?

Only time would tell.

MOTHER AND STEP-FATHER Mrs. Genevieve Fields and Mr. Sam Fields, leave the Metropolitan Methodist Church following the formal services of Dr. Russell H Carrington Jr.

LEAVING THE FUNERAL SERVICE from the Metropolitan
Methodist Church are Dr. Russell H. Carrington Jr.'s father &
Step-Mother Mr. Russell H. Carrington Sr. and Mrs. Evelyn
Carrington

LEAVING THE FUNERAL of Dr. Russell H. Carrington Jr. is Ex-wife Francis Lokeman and son Russell H Carrington III

Letter to my Grandfather

Hello Grand Dad,

I understand all is not well; giving the time you left us. I'm sure you know that your father also left us shortly after you. You guys have probably had discussions by now.

I've been told, that I have a lot of your mannerisms, so I'm sure you will not mind me being direct. I'm going to get directly to the point. Everyone is gone now and my dad is living around the corner from you in heaven. He is still mad at you, so no need to go visit!

Although, we only had the opportunity to meet once. I want to know, if you considered all that you left behind. Your oldest son, my dad, struggled really bad with abandonment issues and depended on illegal drugs for most of his adult life. I wonder if his life would be different if you were still here.

Moreover, I know it's widely discussed how you didn't include my dad in your 'Will" or "Estate." Why? Was that your way of control or just your selfishness? He was well taken care because you picked well with his mother. You left two other sons here, but no one wanted to take up this task of writing this letter.

I'm the fourth generation of Carrington's. I'm taking a shot at restoring your character and applaud your great achievements. You deserve that. You worked hard at that. By, no means are we condoning your actions, but your brilliance cannot be denied. My father has given me all his insight into this biography.

All of your physician partners from Garwyn Medical Center are in heaven with you. Barbara Ann, my Grand mother Frances, and most of all Johnnie Mae are all living in heaven now. You owe them all a big apology for your actions. After, you finished your apology...

Rest in Peace!

Russell H Carrington IV

About the Author

Russell H. Carrington IV is the grandson of Dr. Russell Carrington Jr., a pioneering Black oral surgeon whose life inspired this biographical drama. Born and raised in Baltimore, Maryland, Russ Carrington IV grew up hearing whispered legends and cautionary tales about the man behind the title "Doctor"—a man both revered and resented within the family. Drawing on oral histories, legal records, private letters, and community lore, he set out to uncover the truth buried beneath a polished legacy.

A writer, Real Estate Developer, and community advocate, Russ Carrington IV brings generational insight to The Perfect Smile, peeling back the layers of ambition, silence, and familial sacrifice. This is not just the story of a man—it is the *reckoning of a lineage.*

www.russcarringtoniv.com

A Call To Action – "Beyond the Smile"

The Perfect Smile is more than a story—it's a mirror. Behind Dr. Russell Carrington Jr.'s polished exterior was a man battling invisible wars: between duty and desire, success and selfhood, legacy and loneliness.

To every Black man reading this:

You don't have to carry it all in silence.

You don't have to earn love through pain.

You don't have to break yourself to build something lasting.

Talk to someone. A therapist, a mentor, a brother.

Feel something. Not just the wins—but the grief, the pressure, the need for rest.

Heal. Because survival is not the end goal—wholeness is.

Let The Perfect Smile be a starting point.

Not for pretending—but for confronting. For reclaiming your joy, your peace, your power.

Your life is not just a legacy. It's a life. Live it.

Thanks for reading! Please add a short review on Amazon and let me know what you thought!

www.ingramcontent.com/pod-product-compliance
Lightning Source LLC
LaVergne TN
LVHW051415080426
835508LV00022B/3100